MW01405871

Western Frontiersmen Series
XXXIII

Sacagawea's Child

The Life and Times of Jean-Baptiste (Pomp) Charbonneau

by
SUSAN M. COLBY

THE ARTHUR H. CLARK COMPANY
Spokane, Washington
2005

copyright © 2005 Susan M. Colby
ISBN 0-87062-339-7

All rights reserved including the rights
to translate or reproduce this work or parts
thereof in any form or by any media.

THE ARTHUR H. CLARK COMPANY
P.O. Box 14707
Spokane, WA 99214

Library of Congress Cataloging-in-Publication Data
Colby, Susan M.
  Sacagawea's child : the life and times of Jean-Baptiste (Pomp)
Charbonneau / by Susan M. Colby.
    p. cm. — (Western frontiersmen series ; 33)
  Includes bibliographical references and index.
  ISBN 0-87062-339-7 (alk. paper)
  1. Charbonneau, Jean-Baptiste, 1805–1866. 2. Sacagawea—Family. 3. Lewis and Clark Expedition (1804–1806)—Biography. 4. Pioneers—West (U.S.)—Biography. 5. Shoshoni Indians—Biography. 6. Trappers—West (U.S.)—Biography. 7. Frontier and pioneer life—West (U.S.) I. Title. II. Series.
  F592.7.C43C65 2005
  978'.02'092—dc22

                              2004027793

Table of Contents

    Preface 9
    Acknowledgements 13
    Chronology 15
1 Beginnings, Continuities, Character 19
2 The Corps of Discovery 49
3 The Charbonneaus in St. Louis 71
4 The Duke of Württemberg 101
5 Mountain Man 113
6 The Spanish Southwest 139
7 Gold Rush to Trail's End 163
Appendix:
    The Paternal Line of Jean-Baptiste Charbonneau . 183
    Bibliography 185
    Index 197

Illustrations

Fort Mandan.	21
Berge Olivier Charbonneau.	26
The Travellers meeting with Minatarre Indians.	29
Camp of the Kansas Indians at the Blue River.	30
Winter Village of the Minatarees.	46
Journeys of Jean-Baptiste (Pomp) Charbonneau.	48
Sacagawea coins.	57
Pompey's Tower.	63
Buffalo Bull Dance of the Mandan Indians.	68
Ptihn-Tak-Ochata, Dance of the Mandan.	68
Map of 1822 St. Louis.	82
Monk's Mound.	85
Duke Paul Wilhelm of Württemberg.	100
Former castle of the Teutonic Order in Bad Mergentheim.	111
Trapper's Bride.	135
Buffalo Chase, a Single Death.	144
Mission San Luis Rey.	160
Bar on the Middle Fork of the American River.	168
Sign at gravesite of Jean-Baptiste Charbonneau.	180
Rededication of refurbished site in March 1999.	180

To all the Charbonneau *métis* and
their passion for freedom
And to the Charbonneau heritage
I share with my parents,
Orville Edgar Colby
Jeannette R. Nadon Colby

Preface

Soon after the Columbia River carried Lewis and Clark past present-day Vancouver, Washington, the area became the fur-trading hub for the entire Pacific Northwest. And so, when a woman came to Vancouver to take on the role of Sacagawea and tell the story of this legendary heroine of the Lewis and Clark expedition, many were eager to attend.[1] Following her intriguing performance, a child piped up, "But what happened to your baby? What did Pomp do after they got back?" She told a little of Pomp's story and answered more questions, but others kept bringing the discussion back to the baby boy. They wondered, What kind of a life would such a baby have had? After this heroic start, did he have a heroic life?

The answer is a definite yes! During his adventurous lifespan of sixty-one years, "Pomp," whose real name was Jean-Baptiste Charbonneau, successfully integrated the *voyageur* lifestyle of his father's people, the proud Native American heritage of his mother's people, and the great Jeffersonian traditions of his guardian, William Clark. This unique heritage forged a new kind of American man—a man at ease with the literati of America and Europe, the Mountain Men of the Rockies, and his French and Indian relations in St. Louis and throughout the West. Further-

---

[1] Public lecture/performance given April 13, 2000, by Dakota states historian Jeanne Eder in Vancouver, Wash.

more, Jean-Baptiste remained at the forefront of western expansion his entire life—from his infancy with the Corps of Discovery, to his years as a fur trader and Mountain Man on the upper Missouri and the Santa Fe Trail, to his guidance of the Mormon Battalion and administrative term in southern California, and finally to his gold rush years near Sacramento. A journey through the life of Jean-Baptiste Charbonneau is a journey through the history of Manifest Destiny in the nineteenth century.

My interest in Jean-Baptiste began several years ago when I was researching my own French-Canadian heritage. I found that I descend from three of the children of a seventeenth-century Montreal pioneer, Olivier Charbonneau, and also that Sacagawea's husband, Toussaint Charbonneau, descended from this same pioneer, as did many of the *voyageurs* and other fur traders of the seventeenth through nineteenth centuries. Recently, I discovered that I also descend from Toussaint's maternal line, the Deniaus. I started to think of Jean-Baptiste as one of the many *métis*—children of mixed European and Indian ancestry—and wondered about this very distant cousin of mine. Because of my training in anthropology, I was also interested in his mother's Native American heritage and the effect on his life of trying to reconcile the disparate cultural values of the Indian, French, and Virginian traditions running parallel throughout his life. My research revealed a rich and interesting life, touched on in various publications, but never examined in full.[2]

The Charbonneau/Sacagawea family story has captured

---

[2]The foremost authority on the Charbonneau family was the late Irving W. Anderson, who wrote several biographical summaries of Jean-Baptiste Charbonneau. Other notable biographical summaries were provided by Ann W. Hafen, Charles G. Clark, Albert Furtwangler, Grace R. Hebard, Harold P. Howard, Helen A. Howard, Joyce B. Hunsaker, and W. Dale Nelson, among others. The only full-length biography is by Marion Tinling, but it is written for young adults. See the bibliography for full citations.

the imaginations of so many that it has become legend; as legend, it has slipped at times into myth and off the track of the known facts. Sacagawea has become a stereotype of the compliant Indian maiden, and Toussaint has become a stereotype of the abusive backwoodsman. Jean-Baptiste's life has been seen as ironic—"the gentleman mountaineer." Actually, all three members of this famous family are more complicated, and therefore more interesting, than they are usually portrayed. The best way to understand them is to view them in terms of their own cultures and the realities of their own times. In our times, the term "half-breed," like the term "squaw," has taken on the color of condescension. Therefore, the French term, *métis*, is used here to describe someone of mixed Indian and European heritage.

Scholars have sometimes overly focused on a few controversial details. Is it Tsa-ka-ka-wias, Sacajawea, Sakakawea, or Sacagawea? Did she die as a young woman on the upper Missouri in 1812 or as a centenarian on the Wind River reservation in Wyoming? Did Jean-Baptiste die at Wind River or in Oregon?[3] These questions have merit, but we must not get so caught up in the trees that we lose sight of the forest—that is to say, of their remarkable lives and what those lives tell us about the beginnings of the development of the western United States.

Sometimes we could use a few more trees. There are many gaps in our knowledge of Jean-Baptiste's life. Although he was well educated, he did not write his memoirs; thus, nearly all we know of him comes through the eyes of his contemporaries. Like his mother, however, he made a strong

---

[3]The reader is referred to the most credible research on this topic; see citations for Irving W. Anderson, Kenneth Thomasma, Ann W. Hafen, Donald Jackson, and Harold P. Howard. Other views are presented by Grace Hebard, Thomas Slaughter, and Calvin Grinnell.

impression on those he met, and many of them left provocative glimpses of him over his lifetime. Although we may never be able to know Jean-Baptiste Charbonneau as well as we would like, here is a study of a unique American *métis* and the cultures and times that molded him.

Susan M. Colby
Vancouver, Washington

Acknowledgements

This project grew out of my fascination with seventeenth-century French-Canadian history, which first acquainted me with the remarkable *famille Charbonneau*; and so, I bless the memory of my Uncle Leon Nadon for introducing me to them by fully documenting my mother's genealogy. Thanks also to my cousin, Janice Weisz, who researched my father's side and found Charbonneaus there, too. Historians Jeanne Eder and Barbara Kubik inspired me with their lectures to look beyond Sacagawea, the legend. I am very grateful for inspirational original art generously provided by Carolyn Colby and for the fine map prepared by Salli Hilborn. And *un gros merci beaucoup* to my dear friend, Mary (Marie-Louise) Bennett for providing her research on Charbonneau genealogy, especially for documenting Toussaint's birth and baptismal dates and other genealogical details. Jean-Guy Charbonneau of The Charbonneau Association of Quebec was also very helpful, as was researcher Les W. Branconnier of St. Boniface, Manitoba. My best research resource was the Special Collections Heritage Room of Watzek Library, Lewis and Clark College in Portland, Oregon. Roger Wendlick and the curators, Douglas Erickson and Jeremy Skinner, were always helpful and generous with their time. It was a privilege to have access to the papers there of late Charbonneau family historian Irving W.

Anderson. Staff of Placer County Auburn Library helped me in California, as did Gerald E. Logan, Archivist, Lincoln, California, and my good friend Nancy Minter Bolton. I am grateful to all the museums and libraries that provided illustrations and especially to photographers Keith Hay and Jim Wark. Also, for generously sharing their stories, genealogical data, and photographs, and especially for their support and *joie de vivre*, thank you so much to Eileen Charbonneau and her dear father, Vincent Charbonneau, who died young at the age of eighty-nine. Thank you to Richard Scheuerman for his detailed, constructive comments on my first draft and to the staff of Arthur H. Clark for editorial assistance. I am very grateful to them for this opportunity. And a final thank you to my husband, William Klement Jr., for his editing advice and to all my friends and family for their support and encouragement, especially my mom, Jeannette R. Nadon Colby.

Chronology

1659	Charbonneau family arrives in Montreal from France.
1673	Jacques Marquette and Louis Joliet discover the mouth of the Mississippi.
c. 1720	Horses and European goods arrive in the Rockies from Spanish Southwest.
1738	Chevalier Pierre Gaultier de Varennes and sons are the first whites to meet the Mandans and explore as far as the Rocky Mountains.
1763	Founding of St. Louis by Pierre Laclede Liguest and Auguste Chouteau.
1767	Toussaint Charbonneau born March 20 in Boucherville, Quebec.
c. 1788	Sacagawea born to Lemhi Shoshoni.
1791	Toussaint's father, Jean-Baptiste Charbonneau I, dies in Detroit, June 17.
1792	Captain George Vancouver discovers the mouth of the Columbia River; Alexander Mackenzie crosses the Canadian Rockies to the Pacific.
1793–96	Toussaint works for Northwest Fur Company in Manitoba.
c. 1796	Toussaint settles with Hidatsa in North Dakota.
c. 1800	Sacagawea captured at Three Forks by Hidatsa or Blackfeet and taken east.

1803	Louisiana Purchase in May ratified in October; Toussaint manages Fort Pembina near North Dakota–Manitoba border.
1804	Lewis and Clark begin Corps of Discovery journey May 21, moving into Fort Mandan November 20.
	Toussaint hired November 4.
1805	Jean-Baptiste Charbonneau born February 11 at Fort Mandan, North Dakota.
	Toussaint signs Corps of Discovery contract March 18.
	Charbonneau family embarks with Corps of Discovery April 7.
1806	Jean-Baptiste ill and near death in late May.
	"Pompy's Tower" named in Jean-Baptiste's honor July 25.
	Charbonneaus return to Fort Mandan August 17.
1807–8	Missouri Fur Company formed.
1809	Charbonneaus arrive in St. Louis (probably in autumn).
	Meriwether Lewis dies October 11.
	Jean-Baptiste baptized December 28.
1810	Charbonneaus purchase farmland near St. Louis October 30.
1811	Toussaint and Sacagawea leave St. Louis with Manuel Lisa on April 2.
1812	Toussaint and Sacagawea leave St. Louis with Manuel Lisa in May.
	War of 1812 rages.
	Lizette Charbonneau born about August.
	Sacagawea dies December 20, leaving infant Lizette.

1813–16	Toussaint missing in war; imprisoned in Santa Fe 1815?
1819–38	Toussaint employed by U.S. Indian Department Upper Missouri sub-agency.
1820	Missouri statehood. William Clark loses governorship.
1821	Mexican independence from Spain.
1823	Jean-Baptiste meets Duke Paul, travels to Europe.
1829	Son Anton Fries born February 20 and dies May 15 in Germany; Jean-Baptiste and Duke Paul return to U.S. from Europe.
1830	Jean-Baptiste joins Roubidoux Fur Brigade in the Rockies.
1831	Encounters Joe Meek in winter of 1830–31 in Rockies.
1832	Traps by the skin with Jim Bridger in Rockies.
1833	Traps on the Yellowstone River.
1834	The last year Jean-Baptiste is mentioned on the Upper Missouri.
1834–39	Toussaint at Fort Clark on the Upper Missouri. Jean-Baptiste's whereabouts unrecorded—at Bent's Fort/Santa Fe Trail?
1838	William Clark dies September 1.
1839	Toussaint collects last pay in August and is not heard of again. Jean-Baptiste with Louis Vásquez and Andrew Sublette at Fort Vasquez.
1840	Takes furs east on South Platte River in April; arrives in St. Louis in July.
1841	Encounters Rufus Sage on the White River.
1842	Takes furs east on South Platte River; sees Frémont, Beckwourth, and Sage.

1843	Probable year of Toussaint's death; Jean-Baptiste drives cart west; returns to St. Louis to settle father's affairs.
1844	Hunts at Bent's Fort.
1845	Trailblazes with Fitzpatrick for Lieutenant James W. Abert.
1846–47	Guides the Mormon Battalion.
1847–48	*Alcalde* at Mission San Luis Rey in San Diego area.
1848/49	Travels to northern California; joins gold rush.
1850	Duke Paul visits Sacramento and Fort Sutter; California statehood.
1852	Jean-Baptiste works as assistant-surveyor, Placer County.
pre-1860	Probably works as a runner prior to telegraph.
1861	Works as a clerk at the Orleans Hotel in Auburn, California.
1866	Leaves for Montana; dies May 16 at Inskip's ranch, Danner, Oregon.
1973	Gravesite is declared a Registered National Historic Place March 14.
2001	"Pompey's Pillar" is declared a National Monument January 17.
2005	Jean-Baptiste's two hundredth birthday February 11.

Chapter One

Beginnings, Continuities, Character

... made an addition to our number.
—*Sergeant Patrick Gass*

Jean-Baptiste Charbonneau got off to an auspicious start. His birth was celebrated in no fewer than four separate diaries kept by the members of the Corps of Discovery—those of Lewis, Ordway, Gass, and Whitehouse. Although Captain William Clark was off hunting that winter's day, Captain Meriwether Lewis was present at Fort Mandan for the dramatic birthing ordeal of Sacagawea—a difficult labor, which Lewis himself helped to alleviate. It was on the afternoon of February 11, 1805, that this young mother-to-be struggled in pain:

> About five o'clock this evening one of the wives of Charbono [Sacagawea] was delivered of a fine boy. It is worthy of remark that this was the first child which this woman had borne, and as is common in such cases her labour was tedious and the pain violent; Mr Jessome informed me that he had frequently administered a small portion of the rattle of the rattle-snake, which he assured me had never failed to produce the desired effect, that of hastening the birth of the child; having the rattle of a snake by me I gave it to him and he administered two rings of it to the woman broken in small pieces with the fingers and added to a small quantity of water. Whether this medicine was truly the cause or not, I shall not undertake to determine, but I was informed that she had not taken it more than ten minutes before she brought forth. Perhaps

this remedy may be worthy of future experiments, but I must confess that I want faith as to its efficacy.[1]

It was deep in the North Dakota winter, with the sun setting and the freezing cold closing in, that Jean-Baptiste took his first breaths. From his debut, he was seen by the rugged men around him as "a fine boy." It was his fate to begin and end his remarkable life in the company of adventurous men like these, the men of the Corps of Discovery. It was a common belief in the nineteenth century that the experiences of the mother during pregnancy affected the future choices of the baby. One could certainly make an argument for that belief in this case. Born within Corps-built Fort Mandan, rather than in the Hidatsa dwelling of his parents, it was as though Jean-Baptiste had been predestined for a life that would not be confined to any one culture.

Fort Mandan

After traveling the 1,600 miles from St. Louis to the Mandan villages, Lewis and Clark had just moved into Fort Mandan (near present-day Stanton, North Dakota) on November 20, 1804, less than three months before Jean-Baptiste's birth. On November 2, they had selected a wintering site among the four thousand friendly Mandans and Hidatsas, who were grouped in a confederation of villages more populous than St. Louis. There was no time to waste. The men of the Corps of Discovery immediately set to work in the freezing weather to fell and finish over eight hundred logs of cottonwood, elm, and ash, hauling them all into position and securing them with mud and manure. Afterwards, they constructed the stone fireplaces and erected the tower, gate, and palisade. Hardening themselves for the challenges ahead, they worked long into the frozen nights in order to finish before

---

[1]Reuben Gold Thwaites, ed., *Original Journals of the Lewis and Clark Expedition, 1804–1806*, 1: 257–58.

Fort Mandan. *Courtesy Jim Wark.*

the worst of the winter weather arrived. Soon it would dip as low as forty degrees below zero; some in the Corps, as well as some Indians, would require treatment for frostbite before winter's end. The expedition may well have ended before it began if not for *Sheheke* (White Coyote), the generous civil chief of the Mandan people, who provided them with stored foods when it became too cold to hunt. A true friend, he promised, "If we eat, you shall eat, if we starve, you must starve also."[2]

Just two days after these construction activities had begun, Toussaint Charbonneau approached Lewis and Clark to inquire about accompanying them as an interpreter. Sacagawea was included as well since she might prove useful in interpreting for her tribe, the Shoshoni. Toussaint's friend,

---
[2]Robert Archibald, "Remembering Sheheke: Mandan Chief and American Patriot," 10.

the *métis* interpreter René Jessaume, was already in their employ, and it was Jessaume, rather than a Hidatsa woman, who would deliver this baby, though he may well have been assisted by his Indian wife, a friend of Sacagawea.

Charbonneau-Deniau Family History

Historians have assumed that Toussaint Charbonneau was born around 1759, but genealogical research reveals that he was born in Boucherville, near Montreal, on March 21, 1767, and baptized the next day. Therefore, he was thirty-seven years old when he joined the expedition (not the usually cited forty-six years old). His parents were Jean-Baptiste Charbonneau and Marguerite Deniau, both of Boucherville.[3] Toussaint had his father in mind, and perhaps also his brother Jean-Baptiste, when he named his son.[4]

The Charbonneaus of Boucherville had already been in North America for five generations by the time Toussaint's son was born. The original pioneers had been Toussaint's great-great-grandparents, Olivier Charbonneau and Marie-Marguerite Garnier. This patriarch had been born around 1611 in Marans, Aunis province, in the southwest of France, an area embroiled in the chaos of religious and political wars. After outliving two wives, Olivier married Marie-Marguerite on her twenty-eighth birthday (December 20, 1653). Well past his prime in 1659, he was still bold enough to take a chance in a new land, and so he set out with his extended family for the New World and its uncertainties. Oliver was forty-eight, Marie-Marguerite was thirty-three, and their little girl, Anne, was just two years old when they

---

[3] *Dictionnaire des Mariages Charbonneau*; see also the Appendix and accompanying notes. Toussaint may have represented himself as an older man to gain respect from the Indians, who equated age with wisdom.

[4] Some say Jean-Baptiste was named for a trader/trapper friend of Toussaint, but as Joyce B. Hunsaker points out, it would be more usual in the French-Canadian tradition for a son to be named for his paternal grandfather (*Sacagawea Speaks*, 17).

set sail on *The Saint-André* for the religious colony of Ville Marie (present-day Montreal). Also on board were a number of their relatives and about two hundred other pioneers.[5] This hopeful voyage soon proved disastrous, however, when several of the colonists died of plague before ever reaching New France (present-day Canada). They also had to contend with threatened piracy, terrible storms, and a scarcity of fresh water. It was a long three months before the Charbonneaus finally set foot in Montreal.

Even with its losses, this shipload of new colonists had doubled the population of Montreal, which was then a small village of only 160 citizens. Survival had proven difficult there. Since its founding, just seventeen years prior to the arrival of the Charbonneaus, Ville Marie (named Montreal in 1832) had been under frequent siege from raiding parties of Iroquois coming up from present-day New York state. Many of the early settlers had been killed or taken hostage.[6] As the small band of *habitants* struggled for the survival of the colony, the Charbonneau family endured and proved to be strong and useful citizens. Olivier, a miller who is said to have built the first water mill in Montreal, served the community well for many years. He passed away in 1687 at about the age of seventy-six, which is the same age Toussaint is believed to have reached.

Although founded as a Catholic mission, Ville Marie was in an ideal geographical position to become a hub for the fur trade. Before long, its young men, including Olivier's sons, felt the lure of the West. Keeping their home base in Boucherville, they struck out for unknown lands whenever they got the chance. Toussaint's great-grandfather, Michel Charbonneau, started a long line of fur-trading Charbonneaus that

---

[5]Olivier Charbonneau and Marie Marguerite Garnier, pioneers to Montreal from France in 1659, had five children: Toussaint's ancestor, Michel Charbonneau; Anne, Joseph, Elisabeth, and Jean; for details, see Susan M. Colby, *With Sword, With Cross, With Plough*.
[6]See, for example, Susan M. Colby, "Captives of the French and Indian Wars Part 2: Captured from New France," 133–40.

would eventually include Toussaint and his son.[7] Soon after his father Olivier died, twenty-two-year-old Michel signed on for the western fur trade, and he ended up working for the North West Company for the next thirty-five years. While home during the fall of 1692, he married Marguerite Denoyon, the daughter of Jean Denoyon, a pioneer who had been in the fur-trade as early as 1675. Marguerite was also the sister of the well-known explorer and fur-trader Jacques Denoyon, the first white man to navigate Lake Superior and go as far as Manitoba. Michel, Jacques, and many others like them blazed the trails to the West and established the trade routes and tribal relationships from which Lewis and Clark would benefit more than a hundred years later.[8]

---

[7]Toussaint's great-grandfather, Michel Charbonneau, hired on in the fur trade for *8ta8ats* in 1688, at the age of twenty-two. Michel's father-in-law, Jean Denoyon, had hired on in 1675 for *Outauais* [Ottowa]. Toussaint's maternal great-grandfather, Jacques Reguindeau, went west twice, in 1694 and 1695, at age twenty-one and twenty-two. Michel's eldest brother Joseph Charbonneau, went west in 1698. These two brothers signed on for Detroit in 1707. Joseph, or his son Joseph, went again to Detroit in 1708 (Anne L. Faulkner, "A Tribute to Alphonse Sierens," editor's note, 43). Other early Charbonneaus in the fur trade include a later Joseph to Lac-des-Bois (east of Winnipeg) in 1735, Pierre to *Kamanitigouilla* in 1738, and Jacques to Grand Portage (at the easternmost tip of Minnesota, the final destination for part-timers) in 1756. A copy of the death record for Toussaint's father, Jean-Baptiste Charbonneau, from Saint Anne's Parish in Detroit, is in the possession of the author. "The symbol '8' that appears in the names of the Native signatories is derived from a phonetic symbol first used by the Jesuits and the French to approximate a Native consonant sound close to the 'W' in Wendat, Wentsiwan, etc. The actual [handwritten] manuscript symbol consists of a Greek epsilon combined with a Greek omega, thus the 'open' appearance of the '8' in the facsimile of the signatures. As typographers of the time had no way of reproducing this symbol, they replaced it with the number 8, which, in turn, eventually made its way into manuscript usage" (Havard, *The Great Peace*, 215).

[8]Several Frenchmen had blazed the trail for Lewis and Clark in the eighteenth century. In 1738, Chevalier Pierre Gaultier de Varennes, Sieur de la Verendrye, and his sons were the first white men to meet the Mandans: their expedition went as far as Shoshoni country (a lead tablet left by La Verendrye in Pierre, South Dakota, was found by a schoolgirl there in 1913). La Verendyre was aware of the sea to the west but did not cross the Rockies because of deaths in his party. His expedition built forts all along the way that kept the British at bay, and also served to keep the field open for Lewis and Clark and the United States. There were already many French place names, structures, and farms in what is now Kansas long before Lewis and Clark passed through. "The standard label for the Lewis and Clark expedition might with more fairness be expanded to 'Lewis and Clark and Verendrye and Drouillard and Charbonneau'" (Charles E. Hoffhaus, "French made Lewis and Clark expedition successful").

Michel Charbonneau's son, also named Michel, married Genevieve Babin (also called Lacroix and Richaume) and this couple would become Toussaint's grandparents. Their son, Jean-Baptiste Charbonneau, Toussaint's father, died in Detroit in 1791, perhaps on fur trade business. In spite of all their wanderings over the generations, Boucherville had remained the home base of the clan for one hundred years. It was there that three generations of Charbonneaus had been born before him, and it was there that Toussaint, as well, was born that spring day in 1767.

Although Toussaint's mother, Marguerite Deniau, is sometimes described as Native American, genealogical research shows that she, too, was French.[9] Like the pioneer Charbonneaus of the seventeenth and eighteenth centuries, the Deniaus had a long history in Montreal. The pioneer founder of the family, Jean Deniau (Toussaint's maternal great-great-grandfather) had arrived in New France from Brittany in 1663, just four years after the pioneer Charbonneaus. He had married Hélène Daudin in 1664, and together they struggled to survive the relentless Iroquois raids. Unhappily, these Deniau pioneers were not as fortunate as the pioneer Charbonneaus. Both Jean and Hélène Deniau were killed in a raid on their home on August 12, 1695. Their children did survive, however, and one of the six, Pierre Deniau, became Toussaint's maternal great-grandfather. Like the Charbonneaus, many Deniaus went west in the fur trade, but (at least, in Toussaint's line), they always returned in order to marry and raise their families in Boucherville.

---

[9]Some say Toussaint's mother was a Sioux but I have been unable to discover any Indian heritage in his genealogy—his mother's Deniau family line has been traced back to France. Frenchmen were encouraged to marry Indians only if they would become Catholics and live with the colonists as French women, but such marriages were extremely rare as the native women wanted to stay with their own people. Since all of Toussaint's ancestors lived in and around Boucherville, Quebec, and none were identified as Indians in the records, it is not likely that any of them were Indians. *Dictionnaire des Mariages Charbonneau.*

Berge Olivier Charbonneau, a park on Laval Island, just north of Montreal Island, named for the pioneer ancestor of Toussaint and Jean-Baptiste Charbonneau. *Photo by Susan Colby.*

Toussaint Charbonneau Goes West

Breaking with the traditions of his ancestors, Toussaint left home in his twenties and never returned to settle down. While growing up, he must have heard many family stories about going west, especially about the adventures of his great-grandfather, Michel Charbonneau, and the North West Company. At some point Toussaint decided that this was the life for him, too. Perhaps he had accompanied his father to the fur-trading hub of Detroit and was with him in 1791 when he died there. Although we do not know why his father was in Detroit or if Toussaint was with him, just two years later, Toussaint is found in the West and working for the North West Company. Their records show him at Pine Fort on the Assiniboine River in Manitoba from 1793 to

1796.[10] Since this was the southernmost post of the North West Company, its range had to extend far to the south to serve tribes like the Mandan and Gros Ventre (Hidatsa).[11]

In 1803, Toussaint was associated with the American Fur Company at Fort Pembina on the present-day North Dakota–Manitoba border, which he and Alexander Henry (the younger) were managing together. The following year, when he met Lewis and Clark, he was working as an interpreter, having settled in the second of the three Hidatsa villages on the Knife River, the one called "the little village" (also called *Metaharta* or *Awatixa*).

This western wilderness, once considered part of New France, was part of the vast, uncharted lands of the Northwest with no international border. French was spoken throughout the region and was the language of towns like St. Louis and New Orleans. Father Jacques Marquette and Louis Joliet had discovered the mouth of the Missouri in 1673, and French-Canadian explorers and traders had followed, penetrating a thousand miles or more up the Missouri by the late 1760s. Although owned by Spain when Toussaint arrived, the culture had remained French, and it was French passports that Lewis and Clark carried on their journey. This Louisiana Territory west of the Mississippi and extending to

---

[10] Irving W. Anderson, "A Charbonneau Family Portrait," 11. Annie H. Abel, ed., (*F.A. Chardon, Chardon's Journal at Fort Clark, 1834–1839*, n.258), citing the journal of John MacDonell, 1793–1795, details Toussaint's activities during that period.

[11] The Mandan and Hidatsa are separate tribes within the Siouan language family, but they were closely associated. At the time of Lewis and Clark, there were two Mandan and three Hidatsa villages in proximity along the Missouri. Jointly numbering about four thousand, they had come together for defense against the Teton Sioux. Confusion arises with the term "Gros Ventre" since it is has been used to designate two unrelated groups—the Algonkian-speaking Arapaho, called "Gros Ventres of the Prairie," and the Siouan-speaking Hidatsa (called Minitaree by the Mandan), with whom Lewis and Clark wintered. The latter are sometimes called "Gros Ventres of the Missouri." See Roger C. Owen, James J. F. Deetz and Anthony Fisher, *North American Indians: A Sourcebook*, and James P. Ronda, *Lewis and Clark among the Indians*, for more details about these tribes.

the Rockies had only just been purchased by America in 1803 (after passing from Spanish back to French hands in 1800). Toussaint was far less foreign in this part of the world than were Lewis and Clark and their English-speaking contingent. The captains relied upon this rich legacy, provided by the French fur traders and explorers, for their maps and lines of communication, and were pleased when Corps member George Drouillard was able to recruit seven experienced French boatmen, familiar with the river and the tribes.[12]

Family Portrait

There are no well-documented likenesses of Toussaint or his family. There is a painting by Karl Bodmer, said by a noted Charbonneau family scholar, Irving W. Anderson (1992), to include a probable likeness of Toussaint. In it, he is depicted as clean-shaven and taller than Prince Maximilian of Wied, who was of medium height. Yet Harold P. Howard pictures him as "short, swarthy, and bearded, talkative, perhaps boastful,"[13] while Gordon Speck imagines him as "medium height and heavily built, with brown eyes, a swarthy skin, and a face adorned with a huge mustache."[14] But all this is speculation. Although the stereotype portrays the French-Canadian as dark and "swarthy," most of those who have no Indian admixture (as was the case for Toussaint) are mainly of Norman ancestry and have fair com-

---

[12]For example, Lewis carried an English translation of a book by French engineer-historian Le Page Du Pratz, *Histoire de La Louisane*, on which he relied a great deal (Charles E. Hoffhaus, "French made Lewis and Clark expedition successful," *Kansas City Star*, Oct. 10, 13, and 18, 1980). Lewis also used maps by Antoine Soulard, surveyor-general of Upper Louisiana for the Spanish, which proved to be remarkably accurate (Ann Rogers, *Lewis and Clark in Missouri*, 21–22; Ronda, *Lewis and Clark among the Indians*, 10, 13). Fur trader Régis Loisel was able to give them information about the current situation on the Missouri as far as South Dakota (Rogers, *Lewis and Clark in Missouri*, 35–36). Also see Rogers, *Lewis and Clark in Missouri*, 27, as to the men Drouillard recruited to accompany the expedition to the Mandan villages.
[13]Harold P. Howard, *Sacajawea*, 164.   [14]Gordon Speck, *Breeds and Half-Breeds*, 97.

The Travellers meeting with Minatarre Indians near Fort Clark,
by Karl Bodmer. Toussaint is believed to be the man right
of center who is pointing at Prince Maximilian.
Engraving with aquatint, hand-colored (Vignette XXVI).
Courtesy of Joslyn Art Museum, Omaha, Nebraska.

plexions. Years of living in the elements, however, may well have turned his skin brown and leathery.

As for Jean-Baptiste, there is only one known painting which may depict his likeness. It was located and photographed by Friedrich Bauser in Germany at the request of Grace Hebard for her 1932 book about Sacagawea. The focal point of the painting is Duke Paul of Württemberg, seated in a forest, surrounded by several partially-clothed Indians, one of whom wears a large hat. Also present are three fully-clothed men, two of whom stand near the duke, with the third lounging with Indians off to the side. Hebard decided that one of the Indians, the one seated near Paul holding a peace pipe, was Jean-Baptiste. A recent re-interpretation by

Camp of the Kansas Indians at the Blue River, on the 3rd July 1823. Chiefs Wakan-zie and Sa-ba-no-sche, by Duke Paul of Württemberg. *From* Sacajawea: A guide and interpreter of the Lewis and Clark expedition, with an account of the travels of Toussaint Charbonneau, and of Jean-Baptiste, the expedition papoose, by Grace Raymond Hebard (*Glendale, Calif.: The Arthur H. Clark Company, 1933*). Arrow added to identify Jean-Baptiste.

Stuttgart researcher Monika Firla[15] argues against this and suggests that the clothed, bearded figure directly behind the prince may be Jean-Baptiste. This figure does have the slender build of a young man, but would a half-Indian lad, barely eighteen, already have such a full beard with big muttonchops?[16] One clue is Duke Paul's own account of his first

---
[15] Albert Furtwangler, "Sacagawea's Son New Evidence from Germany," *Oregon Historical Quarterly* 102, no. 4: 518. Furtwangler argues that it was drawn by Duke Paul of Württemberg. He explains that this lithograph was incorrectly attributed by Grace Hebard in *Sacajawea* to Balduin Möllhausen. The original painting hangs in the Deutschordensmuseum in Bad Mergentheim, Germany. The lithograph version, owned by a private collector, bears a title in German, which Furtwangler translates as "Camp of the Kanzas at the Blue River, the 3rd of July 1823. Chiefs Wakan-zie and Sa-ba-No-sche."

[16] Most Indian men have little facial hair. Further, Francis Parkman (*The Oregon Trail*, 169) found that the Indians also had a higher opinion of clean-shaven men.

meeting with Jean-Baptiste, where he twice refers to him as a youth of sixteen. This suggests the lad was not bearded but small and boyish-looking. I believe that Jean-Baptiste may be the young man standing alone on Duke Paul's right and facing him, dressed only in briefs and a large hat (unlike what the Kansas Indians or the white men are wearing). Since he had been living with the Indians for some time, it seems likely that this *métis* lad would be dressed comfortably for a summer day, somewhat in the manner of the Indians, while the visitors would be more formally attired.

Toussaint's Image

We can only imagine how Toussaint, Sacagawea, and Jean-Baptiste might have looked. Keep in mind that popular stereotypes of them have often proven to be in error, depending, as they do, upon the preconceptions of the writer. Grossly biased assessments, not just of appearance, but also of character, have been passed on over the years with little scrutiny. The image most have of Toussaint was formed in 1893 by one of the editors of the Lewis and Clark journals, Elliot Coues. Not only did Coues call Toussaint a coward and wife-beater, but his repeated vitriolic language and extreme sarcasm reveal a hatred beyond all comprehension for someone whom he had never met. As Lange, Speck, and others point out, the evidence for this harsh assessment, in the words actually written by Lewis and Clark, is slim.[17]

The charge of cowardice was based on Toussaint's panic (as a non-swimmer) when faced with drowning[18] and on his

---

[17]See, for example, Ronda, *Lewis and Clark among the Indians*; Robert E. Lange, "Poor Charbonneau! Was He As Incompetent As The Journals/Narratives Make Him Out To Be?"; Dennis R. Ottoson, "Toussaint Charbonneau, A Most Durable Man"; Irving W. Anderson, "A Charbonneau Family Portrait"; Hunsaker, *Sacagawea Speaks*; Speck, *Breeds and Half-Breeds*; Rita Cleary, "Charbonneau Reconsidered"; H. P. Howard, *Sacajawea*; Olin D. Wheeler *The Trail of Lewis and Clark, 1804–1806*; Bernard DeVoto, *Across the Wide Missouri*. [18]Thwaites, *Original Journals*, 2: 34–35.

retreat into the bushes when surprised by a grizzly bear,[19] neither of which struck his fellow Corpsmen as cowardly under the circumstances. The charge of wife-beater was based on one journal entry where Lewis wrote, "I checked our interpreter for Stricking [sic] his woman at their dinner."[20] This behavior in the presence of the captains may well have been Toussaint's way of testing their reactions. Was he demonstrating his prowess to his leaders? Such behavior was expected in Toussaint's circle, where some men believed that an Indian wife needed "sound lashings to keep alive her respect and affection."[21] When Lewis and Clark made it clear, however, that they would not tolerate wife-beating, there was no repetition. Likewise, Toussaint's alleged boasting was also consistent with prevailing values. In many tribes, an Indian would greet another with a recital of past achievements. But where are the examples of such boasting by Toussaint? There is, on the other hand, at least one example of Toussaint apologizing for his failings; he admitted to Prince Maximilian that, even after all his years speaking the language, he still had trouble pronouncing Hidatsan Sioux correctly.[22]

Why, then, did Coues repeatedly damn Toussaint in his footnotes, going so far as to revile Clark for bothering to save Toussaint's life?[23] The most telling reason is seen in

---

[19]Ibid., 2: 109.   [20]Ibid., 2: 349.

[21]Ray Mattison, "The Upper Missouri Fur Trade: Its Methods of Operation," 22, citing Kurz's journal, 155.

[22]See, for example, Parkman, *The Oregon Trail*, 12–13, as to Indian boasting. For Toussaint's apology to Prince Maximilian, see R.G. Thwaites, ed., "Maximilian, Prince of Wied, Travels in the Interior of North America," 23: 223.

[23]Elliot Coues, ed., *Meriwether Lewis and William Clark The History of the Lewis and Clark Expedition*, 2: 442, n.30: "On most occasions Captain Clark showed himself possessed of rare judgement and fortitude. Today, however, he was not up to the mark, and the cowardly wife-beating tenderfoot still lived. The latter may serve to remind one regretfully of the boy's definition of 'amphibious,' as something that could not live on land and died in the water." Although Charbonneau had at least twelve years' experience by then, Coues, smugly nestled in his armchair by the fireside, calls him "tenderfoot."

Coues' choice of words, describing Toussaint as "that craven French apology for a male."[24] It was the long and deep-seated ethnic animosities in the East between the French and the English, following several brutal wars, that informed his biased views. It is likely, too, that Jean-Baptiste encountered this same prejudice as the British-Americans moved west. In 1846, Parkman noted that "the emigrants felt a violent prejudice against French Indians, as they called the trappers and traders."[25] Those who had Indian as well as French blood suffered even more since the emigrants did not want "half breeds" settling among them as property owners. Even the "well-behaved, normally educated, half-breed majority suffered many rebuffs and much mental anguish."[26]

There are many incidents that contradict Coues' assessment. Toussaint's bravery in the War of 1812 clearly refutes any charge of cowardice. Also, in 1833 Toussaint was described as "more sagacious than his overlords—in fact, he saved Maximilian from robbery—and could travel river or prairie forever, winter or summer."[27] Aside from guiding and linguistic skills, Prince Maximilian was also grateful for Toussaint's ethnographic insights about the tribes they encountered.[28] As to cowardice, in June 1836, Major Mitchell reported that Toussaint received two balls through the

---

[24]Coues, *Meriwether Lewis and William Clark*, 1: 310–11, n.28 and 29.
[25]Francis Parkman, *The Oregon Trail*, 92. This prejudice also kept French-Canadians from becoming American culture heroes. Kit Carson's biographer makes the point that Kit was no better than several others (mainly French) in Frémont's employ, but it was Kit who became the household name, as his Anglo image and heritage embodied American ideals. (Harvey L, Carter, "Kit Carson," 190.)
[26]Harvey E. Tobie, "Joseph L. Meek," 366.
[27]DeVoto, *Across the Wide Missouri*, 134.
[28]Thwaites, ed., "Maximilian Prince of Wied, Travels in the Interior of North America." Others for whom Toussaint worked who spoke favorably of him included François Antoine Lacrocque of the North West Company (Leroy R. Hafen, ed., *The Mountain Men and the Fur Trade of the Far West*, 9: 60).

hat in an Indian skirmish.[29] Even in such circumstances, he never carried a gun himself, relying instead on his knife.[30]

Less easy to refute, on the other hand, is the assessment of Toussaint as an abuser of women—neither because of his relationship with Sacagawea, nor because of his tendency to accumulate wives, but because of one alleged incident of sexual assault as a young man working in Manitoba.[31] As to the polygamy, it is true that by 1805, Toussaint had taken at least one other Shoshoni wife in addition to Sacagawea, and possibly a Mandan wife as well. It is also well-documented that he took even more wives over the years—at least two in his years at Fort Clark and one more in his old age. At that time, however, polygamy was a common practice among these tribes, and a great many fur traders were not averse to marriage *à la façon du pays* (according to the customs of the country). Such polygamy was not confined to the traders. Often the head agents, typically gentlemen from respected eastern families, took one or more Indian wives, both for convenience and in order to forge alliances with Indian chiefs. Occasionally, these Indian families were taken east, but usually they remained with their western tribes, separate from their white counterparts.

---

[29]Stella Drumm, ed., *Journal of a Fur-trading Expedition on the Upper Missouri 1812–1813 by John C. Luttig*, 139, citing a letter from Major D. D. Mitchell to W. N. Fulkerson, Indian agent for the Mandans.

[30]Ibid., Appendix 137.

[31]Abel (*F.A. Chardon*, 270–71, n.258) citing John MacDonell's journal for May 30, 1795: "Tousst Charbonneau was stabbed at the Manitou-a-banc end of the PlP [Portage la Prairie] in the act of committing a Rape upon her Daughter by an old Saultier woman with a Canoe Awl—a fate he highly deserved for his brutality—It was with difficulty he could walk back over the portage." This journal was accessed by Abel from photostats, *Masson Papers*, Public Archives, Ottawa. W. Dale Nelson (*Interpreters with Lewis and Clark*, 13) suggests, on the other hand, that MacDonell was prejudiced against all free traders, calling them *canaille* (riffraff), so he may have exaggerated the incident. LeRoy R. Hafen (*The Mountain Men*, 9: 58) mentions a dubious claim by a mulatto of ill repute, Edward Rose, who said that, in about 1814, he and Charbonneau carried out a plan to purchase Arapaho women to sell to traders as wives.

According to Prince Maximilian, the Indian nicknames for Toussaint included "the chief of the little village, the man who possesses many gourds, the great horse from abroad, the forest bear, and fifth, which, as often happens among these Indians, is not very refined."[32] Harold P. Howard adds that "these names were bestowed in mockery, but not necessarily in antagonism."[33] He and others concede that Toussaint would not have been allowed to live among these tribes for so many years if he had not been seen as a friend and an asset. Over time, Toussaint augmented his skills, adding English and more Indian languages to his linguistic accomplishments. That he worked his way up from a greenhorn *engagé* (hired hand) to interpreter, fur-trader, and fort manager and was able to consistently command high wages from $300 to $400 per year speaks well of his abilities and his usefulness over his long career. In sum, Toussaint Charbonneau was accepted by the Indians as a go-between. Not an Indian or an Anglo, he was someone who could connect the two to the advantage of both—that is, he was a French-Canadian trader, guide, and interpreter with the skills, endurance, and cunning required for that demanding life. He was unlettered, rough around the edges, and impulsive. At times, he was violent and opportunistic. He was typical of his lot— not fit for the drawing room, but very fit to drive hard bargains with tough-dealing trading partners and to live to tell about it. Such traits were disdained by those with European standards of how a man should present himself. Soft gentlemen of English heritage living in the cities of New England,

---

[32]Speck, *Breeds and Half-Breeds*, 138, provides this 1832 quote from the journal of Prince Maximilian; also see Thwaites, "Maximilian Prince of Wied," 23: 221. Parkman (*The Oregon Trail*, 225) gives an example of how Indians bestowed unrefined nicknames in fun. The use of ironic *dit* names (nicknames or *noms de guerre*) was popular among French-Canadians as well.

[33]H. P. Howard, *Sacagawea*, 164 (also see 15, 17, 163–68).

like Elliott Coues, who disliked the French on principle, would judge him harshly (and, unfortunately, Coues' prejudices have colored most of the subsequent portrayals of Toussaint), but men like William Clark, who understood life in the untamed West and respected those who survived and succeeded there, would come to value him highly.[34]

Sacagawea's Heritage

Of course, the roots of the baby's mother went even deeper into the history of this land. Sacagawea's name is much better known than that of her husband or of her son, and it is not surprising that her romantic story has captured the imagination of generations.[35] Although there are no actual pictures or descriptions of her, most Americans have a mental image of her and recall, from their school days, the basic tale of her origins. She was born a Shoshoni in the Rocky Mountains, but was kidnapped by Hidatsa when she was between ten and thirteen years old and taken as a slave to the village where Lewis and Clark encountered her in 1804. By then, she was about sixteen years old. She had been purchased or won in a gambling game by Toussaint Charbonneau and was carrying his child. Her story is far more complex than this simple summary, however.

Just as Toussaint Charbonneau is better understood when seen in terms of his French Canadian heritage and the trappers' culture, so it is that Sacagawea, too, must be placed in the context of her background, which was already quite complicated by the time she met Lewis and Clark. She had been

---

[34] Thwaites *Original Journals*, 2: 497.
[35] See Irving W. Anderson and Blanche Schroer ("Sacagawea Her Name and Destiny," 8–9) for a discussion of the spelling of Sacagawea's name. The spelling used here is that currently accepted by most Lewis and Clark scholars, the U.S. Geographic Names Board, the U.S. National Park Service, the National Geographic Society, The Bureau of American Ethnology, and several encyclopedias.

born to the Shoshoni, raised as a Hidatsa adoptee, and married off to a Frenchman—all before reaching her late teens. Her short life had been about adjusting to change and making the most of it. She had seen violent death and suffered the terrors of kidnapping and separation from family. She had had no control over what happened to her. Yet her gentle nature and fine character had endured and she won the respect and admiration of all who had written of her.

How could this be? The answer to understanding Sacagawea's nature is found in a study of her heritage and early days. Her people are variously referred to as Shoshoni, Shoshone, Lemhi, Grass Lodges, Mountain Snakes, Salmon Eaters, and *Agaideka* (*Agaidüka*).[36] Most Shoshonis lived in the desert and plateau regions, not in the mountains where Sacagawea was born. Her people were the most northerly members of the Northern Shoshoni tribe, which has been called "the most prominent and strongest tribe of the upper plateau."[37] Sacagawea's branch, called the *Agaideka*, lived at the interface of the Plains, the Great Basin, and the Plateau cultures in Montana and Idaho. Although categorized as a Plains Culture, they were not typical of that group, since they combined the skills achieved over the millennia by their Shoshoni fisher/gatherer forebears of the Plateau and Great Basin with the bison-hunting skills of the Plains tribes.[38]

Sacagawea was raised in an egalitarian society where individuals were valued on merit and each person retained much independence. Children, especially the boys, were seldom punished, as the Shoshoni feared this humiliation would break the child's spirit and rob him of his confidence and feel-

---

[36] Brigham D. Madsen, *Lemhi: Sacajawea's People*; John R. Swanton, *The Indian Tribes of North America*. The spelling used here, *Shoshoni*, is that recognized in the *Handbook of American Indians North of Mexico*, 2 volumes, published by the Bureau of American Ethnology, Washington, D.C., 1910, vol. 2: 1139.
[37] Swanton, *The Indian Tribes of North America*, 404.
[38] Owen *et al.*, *North American Indians*, 492.

ing of independence.[39] Leaders, like her brother Cameahwait, were not hereditary chiefs, but were chosen to lead the tribe in war and hunting because of their personal generosity, wisdom, bravery, and skill. These chiefs did not decide matters unilaterally but consulted with councils of lesser chiefs and other distinguished men.[40] Lewis and Clark's style of leadership in which they consulted fellow Corps members on key issues must have felt normal and natural to Sacagawea.

An adaptable people, Sacagawea's birth tribe traditionally used various ecological zones in a seasonal round. They traveled to the prairies and meadows in the spring to gather greens and camas bulbs. Women were adept at gathering over one hundred different species of wild plants, a skill that would come to serve the Corps of Discovery well during lean times.[41] By summer there was salmon fishing, and bison hunting and berry picking on the Plains occupied the late summer and fall. Winter was spent on the Lemhi River, where they had access to wood and water and were protected from storms but were still close enough to the mountains to hunt for game. Depending on seasonal needs, they would travel in small bands or with much larger groups, including Flatheads and Nez Perce, covering an expansive area including the Lemhi Valley, some of the upper Missouri country, and across the Continental Divide. Since they were at the interface of three diverse ecozones, trade was also an important part of their economic strategy.

This melding of traditions was relatively recent in Sacagawea's time. Major disruptions had followed the arrival of foreign goods and the horse from Spanish New Mexico, and both introductions were radically changing traditional cul-

---

[39]Nelson, *Interpreters with Lewis and Clark: The Story of Sacagawea and Toussaint Charbonneau*, 42.
[40]Robert F. and Yolanda Murphy, "Shoshone-Bannock Subsistence and Society," 334.
[41]Owen et al., *North American Indians*, 244.

tures by about 1720. Soon it became apparent that those who mastered use of the horse and European weaponry had a major advantage over less mobile tribes, since they could both hunt more effectively and control resource and land use by force. Such a power was the Cheyenne-Arapaho-Sioux alliance formed in the early 1800s. Although the Shoshoni had been among the first tribes of the Northern Plains to adopt the horse, which soon become central to their lives, the Spaniards had refused to provide them with firearms, putting them at a disadvantage for both hunting and protection.[42] As bitter enemies of the Shoshoni, the Plains tribes had forced Sacagawea's people far north of their traditional territory into the mountains. Now, making a living was much harder for the Shoshoni as their competitors restricted their access to the buffalo-rich prairies; therefore, her tribe was suffering in reduced circumstances by the time Sacagawea was born.

When it was time for the buffalo hunt, Sacagawea's people came together with a larger group, both to hunt more effectively and to repulse attacks from Algonkean-speaking Blackfeet and Siouan-speaking tribes, like the Crows. It was a raid by Blackfeet (or by Siouan Hidatsas) to capture horses and captives that swept Sacagawea away in the fall of 1800. She was walking by the river at Three Forks on a gathering foray with others, when suddenly the peace was shattered by raiders on horseback. She ran into the river, trying desperately to escape, but was swooped up mid-river onto the horse of a warrior.[43] Many other Shoshonis, mainly men, were killed that day, but about four of the boys, along with several of the women and girls, including Sacagawea, were carried off.

---
[42]Murphy and Murphy, "Shoshone-Bannock Subsistence and Society," 332.
[43]See John Ordway's journal, June 27, 1805. In Moulton, vol. 9, p. 190.

Sacagawea Among the Hidatsa

There are contradictory versions of what happened next—all poorly referenced, if at all. Lewis and Clark journal editors Biddle and Coues say she was taken in war by the Minnetarees and sold as a slave to Charbonneau, who "brought her up and afterward married her." They apparently deduced this version from William Clark's short reference of November 11, 1804, about "two Squars of the Rock Mountain, purchased from the Indians" by Charbonneau.[44] Speck (1969) sees Sacagawea as a "slave of the vicious LeBorgne, chief of the Minnetarees, when Charbonneau had purchased her some five years previously." Ronda (1983) says that Sacagawea and another Shoshoni girl were purchased by Toussaint between 1800 and 1804, while Hunsaker (2001) does not place Sacagawea with Toussaint until about 1803. A more popular version is one told by Harold Howard, that Sacagawea was kidnapped by raiding Hidatsas and sold to Charbonneau or won by him in a gambling game. (The loser is usually given as Red Arrow.) Both Charles Clark and Donald Jackson have this game taking place in 1794—six years before all other sources say she was captured. Others say she was adopted by the Hidatsa and protected by their customs, and that Toussaint must have given gifts to her family as a dowry in order to take her as a wife. They say that, most likely, he had been required to follow Hidatsa tradition, giving her adoptive family a bride price of two horses, a flintlock rifle, and some calico material, or the equivalent.[45]

---

[44]Coues, *Meriwether Lewis and William Clark*, 1: 257; see Gary Moulton, ed., *The Journals of the Lewis and Clark Expedition*, 3: 232–3.

[45]Coues, *Meriwether Lewis and William Clark*, 1: 257; H. P. Howard, *Sacagawea*, 148; Donald Jackson, ed., *Letters of the Lewis and Clark Expedition with Related Documents 1783–1854*, 147; Hunsaker, *Sacagawea Speaks*; Ronda, *Lewis and Clark Among the Indians*, 256. Jeanne Eder, a Native American, suggests the latter scenario as most likely (public lecture Vancouver, Wash., April 12, 2000). In agreement is Margaret Talbot ("Searching for Sacagawea," 77). On the other hand, Calvin Grinnell, a Hidatsa ("Another View of Sakakawea"), believes (based on tribal oral tradition) that "Sakakawea" was born a Hidatsa.

This last version raises important questions. Was Sacagawea a slave, like the slaves of the South? Was she chattel to be won or lost in gambling games, even as a young girl? Could anyone come along and buy her? Would no one watch out for her welfare? Legends that have formed our present-day opinions of the "Wild West" were formulated by eastern Americans who saw Indians as competitors for land. It was easier to displace them if they were seen as wild savages with no social constraints. They did not understand that Indian tribes had social rules of long-standing just as they did. They knew about the Euro-American slave trade in Africans, but next to nothing about Indian slavery and adoption customs. They assumed that Sacagawea's worth as a slave was only in the profit she could bring—that she had no value to the Indians as a person. We know, however, that the Hidatsa did not practice slavery.[46] Women and children taken in Indian raids were usually seen as replacements for tribal members who had been lost to war and disease. They were adopted in order to take the place of specific family members and treated as though they were the person they replaced. They were not chattel, and when they reached marriageable age, they would be married off according to custom, with their children born free. Only suitors seen as assets to the family would be encouraged, and fur traders were near the top of that list, as they had access to goods from many regions and were good providers. Because of the fur trader's connections, a family could count on extra help in hard times. This was especially true at this crossroads of multi-national commerce where traders could provide luxuries and necessities from "a trade network that faced in three directions and stretched over thousands of miles."[47] Sometimes women were mistreated in these marriages, but in

---

[46] Alfred W. Bowers, *Hidatsa Social and Ceremonial Organization*.
[47] Ronda, *Lewis and Clark Among the Indians*, 75.

most Indian cultures a woman retained the right to return to her father's protection. Often, however, these marriages were tender and met the needs of both parties.[48]

It is not known exactly when or how Sacagawea came to be with Toussaint Charbonneau, and the slave/master relationship presented by legend should not be assumed to be correct. She may not have been "purchased" any more than our own European great-grandmothers were "purchased" when dowries "bought" them. Like too many women in too many places through time and space, Sacagawea did not have much control over her life, but there is no reason to believe she had been dehumanized.[49]

In sum, like many others of her tribe, Sacagawea had been caught up in the conflicts and competitions among the western tribes. In approximately 1800, at about age twelve, she had been taken east by Blackfeet (or by Hidatsas) and adopted by the Hidatsas, who kept her among themselves in *Awatixa* (Metaharta) village, as part of the *Itisuku* clan, and taught her Hidatsa ways.[50] They had determined, sometime between 1800 and 1804, that Toussaint Charbonneau would be her spouse. They knew this would be good for her survival and that of her adoptive family, since, "to become the wife of a fur trader offered the Indian woman the prospect

---

[48]See, for example, Parkman (*The Oregon Trail*, 115–17), who tells of the loving relationship and sorrowful parting of Henry Chatillon and his Indian wife. Also see Sylvia Van Kirk, *Many Tender Ties Women in the Fur Trade Society, 1670–1870*. As to adoption, see Parkman (*The Oregon Trail*, 199–200) for an example of adoptees treated like the person they replaced. Such examples can be found for tribes throughout the East and West.

[49]Some argue that Lewis and Clark's use of the term "squaw," when referring to Sacagawea, was derogatory, but historian Barbara J. Kubik (public lecture, January 24, 2002) states that it probably was not considered as such at the time. She cites the dictionary's derivation of the term from the Algonkian word meaning "woman."

[50]Anderson and Schroer, "Sacagawea Her Name and Destiny," 6, base her age on Lewis's journal entry of July 28, 1805, stating that Sacagawea had been kidnapped "five years hence" and also the August 9, 1805, entry that she had not yet "arrived to the years of puberty . . . 13 or 14 years."

of an alternate way of life that was easier physically and richer in material ways."[51] Rather than a grizzled old man of forty-six, as he is always portrayed, Toussaint was actually in his mid-thirties when Sacagawea became his spouse (and she was about seventeen), and there is no reason to believe that she or her adoptive family found him unattractive or unsuitable.[52]

Shoshoni Child

Although it was traumatic to be taken from her people, in many ways Sacagawea's life was easier with the Siouan-speaking Hidatsa than it would have been had she stayed with her Uto-Aztecan–speaking Shoshoni. Fear of raids, violent death, and unpredictable food shortages dogged the Shoshoni in the days of Sacagawea's youth. Forced into the mountains by powerful Plains tribes, survival was a constant struggle. At certain times of the year, as in summer when Lewis and Clark met them, they lacked food and were needy. Women and children had to work hard. From the age of three, they searched daily for berries, roots, and seeds. Women were also responsible for maintaining fish weirs and gigging salmon with barbed lances, while the men hunted, tended horses, fought enemies, and manufactured and maintained their weapons. Besides child care, cooking, and gathering fish and plants, women had the endless chores of butchering the kill, preparing and storing all food, scraping and curing hides, fabricating clothing, moccasins, bedding, and housing, and carrying loads as they moved from one location to the next; in short, women did nearly all the

---

[51] Van Kirk, *Many Tender Ties*, 6; also see Talbot, "Searching for Sacagawea," 77–78.
[52] The age spread between Toussaint and Sacagawea was nearly identical to that of William Clark and Julia Hancock. A twenty-year difference was not considered excessive or unusual at the time.

"drudgery" required to sustain life.[53] If the men could not hunt because of competition from other tribes and enough plant products could not be found by the women to sustain the group, all soon found themselves in desperate straits.

Meriwether Lewis painted a bleak picture of Shoshoni life as he saw it during that week he spent among them in August 1805.[54] He found them unattractive. The men seemed to him to be lazy since they had only to take care of the horses and hunt, while the women did everything else. The men held the power and their sons were favored, receiving better treatment than their daughters. In fact, according to Lewis, women received little respect. Daughters were for sale and a wife's virtue was not beyond purchase either, although some were held in high esteem. At the same time, however, he saw "every man a chief"—honest, well-behaved, considerate, generous with strangers, brave, poor, but cheerful. This confused assessment is harsh. As Ronda stated, ". . . when dealing with social values and personal relations, he [Lewis] tended to rely on traditional European stereotypes of Indians."[55]

Clark, on the other hand, was more perceptive and catholic when it came to observing other cultures. In his eyes, "The women are held more sacred among them than any nation we have seen and appear to have an equal Shere in all conversation, which is not the Case in any other nation I have seen."[56] Fur trapper Osborne Russell, who spent nine years among them, found the Shoshoni "kind and hospitable to whites thankful for favors indignant at injuries." He noted that decisions were made democratically. Polygamy was common. The women, who performed all the daily work except care of the horses, were "cheerful and affection-

---

[53] Ronda, *Lewis and Clark Among the Indians*, 140, 149.
[54] Moulton, *The Journals of the Lewis and Clark Expedition*, 5: 119–21.
[55] Ronda, *Lewis and Clark Among the Indians*, 148.
[56] Thwaites, *Original Journals*, 3: 10.

ate to their husbands remarkably fond and careful of their children."[57] Unlike Lewis, trapper E. Willard Smith found the Shoshoni "very good looking Indians," the men tall and slight and the women short and stout.[58]

Regardless which of these assessments is closest to the truth, there is no doubt that Shoshoni life was difficult. It is nearly impossible for us today to imagine the challenge of living in the mountains solely by hunting and gathering—facing death by disease, starvation, and warfare on a daily basis, especially during the long, cold winters. Even with great skill and experience, it was a precarious lifestyle, and a particularly difficult one for a woman. It was a life that forged a physically and mentally tough, independent woman. This is why the Lemhi Shoshoni are not as surprised as white Americans by Sacagawea's abilities and manner.[59]

HIDATSA WOMAN

Although, like the Northern Shoshoni, the Hidatsa were also considered part of the Plains cultural group, they too were atypical. Once nomadic, they had settled in with the Mandan for greater security, and this alliance had proved successful for both. These southern Siouan Hidatsa displayed the usual Plains traits but, to this hunter/gatherer base, they had added Mandan agricultural skills. This brought them a more economically secure, sedentary way of life, which included pottery making.[60] They were a prosperous people adept at trading their agricultural products and horses far afield for various European and Indian goods. In

---

[57]Aubrey I. Haines, ed., *Journal of a Trapper: A Hunter's Rambles Among the Wild Regions of the Rocky Mountains, 1834–1843*, Osborne Russell, 143–44.
[58]E. Willard Smith, "Journal," 267, quoted in LeRoy R. and Ann W. Hafen, eds., *To the Rockies and Oregon, 1839–1842*, 155–56.
[59]Kenneth Thomasma, *The Truth About Sacajawea*; see preface by Rod Ariwite.
[60]Owens et al., *North American Indians A Sourcebook*, 1967: 491; Sonja Schierle, ed., *Travels in the Interior of North America*.

Winter Village of the Minatarees. Lithograph by Karl Bodmer. *From* Early Western Travels, 1748–1846, *volume 25, by Reuben Gold Thwaites (Glendale, Calif.: The Arthur H. Clark Company, 1906).*

contrast to the Northern Shoshoni of Sacagawea's youth who dwelled in temporary, cone-shaped brush wickiups, the Hidatsa lived in large, comfortable, hemispherical clay lodges. In the summer, they enjoyed the open breezes of the Missouri and Knife Rivers, and in the winter, they retreated to their forest lodges, which offered fuel and protection from the harsh weather. Sometimes, the buffalo would retreat into the forest as well, seeking respite from the icy storms, giving the hunters an easy hunt.[61]

---

[61]Sonja Schierle, ed., *Travels in the Interior of North America.*

Hidatsa women were highly valued and not limited to a life of drudgery. This was largely because land was passed on in the female line. Since the male line was not important for determining property rights and, thus, paternity was not an essential concern, women were not seen as possessions and they had more sexual and personal freedom. They sought relations with men of power who could pass on this power through procreation.[62] Women also enjoyed considerable prestige since they were in charge of the crops, which were the resources most important to the survival of the tribe. Although it was the men who provided meat and skins from the hunt, their role in tribal survival was secondary to the agricultural role of the women. The fertile riverbanks provided predictable surpluses of corn, beans, squash, and sunflower seeds that could be stored for winter and hard times and traded for other goods. Security was further assured by a vigorous trade with Europeans, conducted by fur traders like Toussaint, who remained in residence. Thus, Sacagawea enjoyed much prestige as the wife of a fur trader in these prosperous villages and as the new mother of a fur-trader's son.

Seeing Sacagawea, then, as a product of her Shoshoni childhood, Hidatsa adolescence, and marriage to a French-Canadian fur trader, it is understandable that she was a confident, accomplished young woman, ready for whatever fate sent her way. Beyond this, however, is the individual temperament with which one is born. Like her brother, who was chosen to be a chief because of his personal qualities, Sacagawea inspired loyalty and devotion, as exemplified by the fact that two gentlemen, with whom she had no ties, later volunteered to take on full responsibility for her children.

---

[62]Ronda, *Lewis and Clark Among the Indians*, 62; Talbot ("Searching for Sacagawea," 78) makes the point that Hidatsa women owned real property at a time when Euro-American women still could not.

Journeys of JEAN-BAPTISTE (POMP) CHARBONNEAU

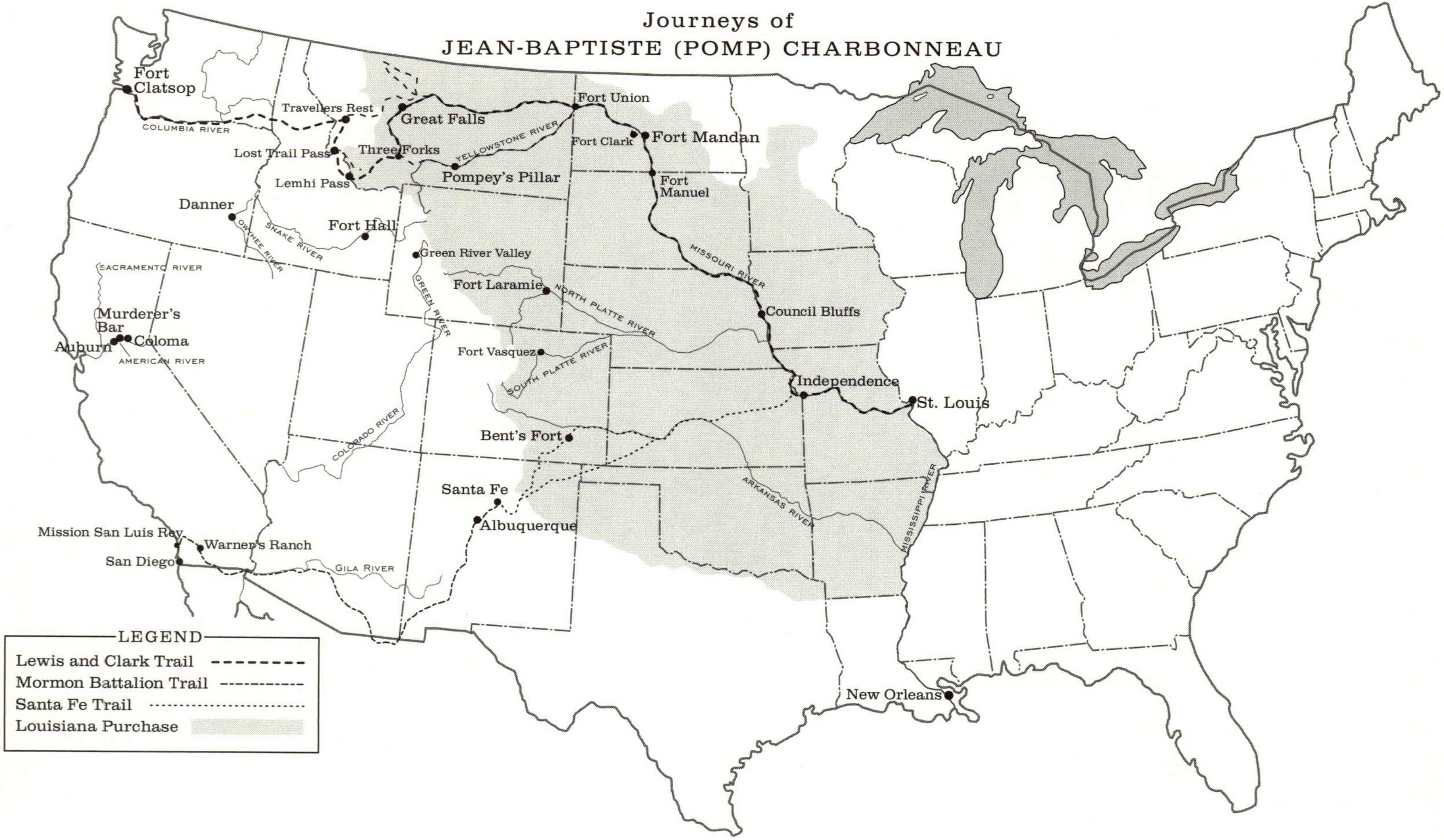

Chapter Two

THE CORPS OF DISCOVERY

In all of American history never has an infant been part of such a major exploration. —*Kenneth Thomasma*[1]

At the age of fifty-five days, Jean-Baptiste Charbonneau set out with his Shoshoni mother, his French-Canadian father, and thirty other intrepid men on the first of his many treks across the country. Most certainly, he was the first person in history to make the 4,356-mile journey on other than his own two feet. The purpose of this historic, heroic journey has been discussed at length by others and will only be touched on here. In brief, President Thomas Jefferson had the foresight to see how advantageous it would be to the nation to purchase the Louisiana Territory from the French; this immense expanse of land was signed over to the United States in Paris in May 1803. Although originally claimed by the French, this land had been in Spanish hands from 1762 until 1800. The Spanish had ruled with such a light touch, however, that the daily lives of the French settlers had barely been affected. Even though Napoleon was able to retrieve this territory from the Spanish in 1800, he soon found that he needed to focus his resources elsewhere. Thus, for only about fifteen million dollars, the United States gained approximately 820,000 square miles of land,

---
[1]Thomasma, *The Truth about Sacajawea*, 86.

extending from the Missouri River as far as the Rocky Mountains. The transfer from Spanish to French to American control was so rapid that all three transactions were ceremonially re-enacted within just one twenty-four–hour period. On March 9, 1804, Lewis and Clark watched, along with the 1,200 citizens of St. Louis, as the Spanish flag was lowered and the French flag was raised. For most, cheers turned to tears the next day, as the French flag was lowered and the American flag was raised.[2]

Jefferson wasted no time as he waited for ratification of the deal by Congress (in October 1803). Having received the approval of Congress earlier that year, he had already begun organizing an expedition to learn all he could about the West. At last, he could put his plan into action. Jefferson was particularly interested in finding a river passage that would allow trade to flow easily across the country. He already knew, from reading French accounts, that the east-flowing Missouri drained a great mountain range; he also knew, from English accounts, that the west-flowing Columbia drained to the Pacific. And he had a rough idea of the distance to the ocean from Alexander Mackenzie's 1801 account of his historic crossing of Canada in 1793. What he longed to discover was a connection or a reasonable portage between these western and eastern river systems. He hoped that the mountains were few and that the Continental Divide would not prove an insurmountable barrier to navigation.

As a man of the Enlightenment, he also wanted to learn as much as possible about the people and resources of the West and how best both could be integrated into the nation. Thus the "Corps of Discovery" came into reality—a multifaceted expedition to blaze a trail for trade, but also to record

---
[2]Stephen E. Ambrose, *Undaunted Courage*, 129.

all new discoveries for the advancement of knowledge. In his wisdom, Jefferson emphasized the importance of making a peaceful impression upon all those encountered. He knew from his own diplomatic experiences in France that successful trade relations depended on trust and goodwill. He insisted that the men going forth to announce the change of dominion and open new trade routes come as friends and bearers of good tidings for the future. He chose the leaders of this crucial mission wisely in his fellow Virginians, Meriwether Lewis, his private secretary, and William Clark, Lewis' trusted, battle-tested friend.

Role of the Charbonneaus

In order to avoid any misinterpretation of their purpose, Lewis and Clark knew that communication was key. They needed interpreters who could communicate with any and all tribes encountered. Sign language would do in many instances, but for important negotiations, especially for obtaining essential survival items and information, spoken language skills were essential. Two of the most important language groups, in particular, would require translators—the Hidatsa/Gros Ventre (Siouan) group and the Shoshoni (Uto-Aztecan) group. Toussaint Charbonneau was adept at the former and Sacagawea at the latter. Since she was born a Shoshoni, they hoped she would be able to negotiate for horses from her people. They knew that horses would be essential for crossing the mountains into the Far West once they had to leave their boats behind. Once past Shoshoni lands, all would be *terra incognita* until they could spot Mt. Hood, the landmark on the Columbia that had been recorded by Englishmen exploring from the Pacific side. This land west of the Rockies was not part of the Louisiana Purchase.

It was unclear if any European power had a legitimate claim to it, but the Spanish, or any number of unknown tribes, could be defending it. If they could communicate effectively with the Shoshoni, perhaps they could learn how best to safely bridge this unknown gap. They also hoped the Shoshoni might know about the navigable connection Jefferson sought.

Toussaint had another Shoshoni wife, and it is not known why this new mother was chosen instead of her. Until shortly before departure, both wives were expected to accompany the Corps, but for unstated reasons, only one went. Sacagawea must have seemed willing[3]—if only to avoid future morale problems, it is doubtful Lewis and Clark would have forced a sullen girl with an infant at her breast onto the trail. Did she hope to be returned to her family? This, too, seems doubtful, since she showed no inclination to be left with the Shoshoni when they were found. What she was feeling on that pleasant spring day, as she climbed into the white pirogue with her seven-week-old infant on her back, we can only imagine. If she ever had regrets, no account of it was ever written. On the contrary, many words were written of her general usefulness and cooperative attitude. Her wilderness skills proved very useful, especially the ability to recognize scores of useful plants that she had learned about as a girl among the adept Shoshoni gatherers. Even though she was so young and this was her first baby and she had no women along to help her, she had to keep up with the men each day and gather food and otherwise make herself useful where needed. Additionally, she had to do her jobs as negotiator and interpreter, as well as nurse, clean, amuse, protect,

---

[3]Moulton, ed., *The Journals of the Lewis and Clark Expedition* 3: 328n, and see Clark's entry April 1, 1805. Perhaps the captains foresaw future difficulties if Charbonneau was accompanied by two wives while the other men had none.

teach, and keep healthy and comfortable a helpless infant. And she had to do it all as they lived in the open in all kinds of terrain and weather.[4]

Hired as an interpreter, a position that placed him above all the men of the Corps but Drouillard, Toussaint did not expect to have extra duties.[5] But this expedition did not have the same traditions as the fur trade. Here he was expected to do whatever needed doing. At first he balked at this and he nearly gave up the job, but he finally acquiesced and signed his contract on March 18. He would wear many hats in the months to come. During the course of the expedition, he would serve as chef, cooking his much-loved specialties (*boudin blanc* being a particular favorite); negotiator for goods and horses; and hunter, scout, horses retriever, and boatman. It was soon too apparent that he was particularly ill-suited for this last job since he was not familiar with boats and did not know how to swim—he tended to panic when the boat faltered, making matters worse. But he performed his other chores competently, and there were even occasions when he sought work from Clark even though he was so incapacitated from various temporary injuries that Clark thought he should not be working at all.[6] Clearly, both husband and wife were assets to the expedition. And Jean-Baptiste did his bit for camp morale too—his trusting innocence calming and softening the rough edges of the trail-weary men. Along with his mother, his very presence was proof of the Corps' peaceful intent, putting the Indians they encountered at ease.[7]

---

[4]H. P. Howard, *Sacajawea*, 149–150. Dr. E. G. Chuinard (*Only One Man Died, The Medical Aspects of the Lewis and Clark Expedition*, 375) reports that the usual native practice was to use skins stuffed with cattail fuzz or moss for diapers.

[5]W. Dale Nelson (*Interpreters with Lewis and Clark*, 7) makes the point that Toussaint was paid the same as Drouillard, which was three to five times more than the other men were paid. Because of their high status, they slept and ate with the captains.

[6]Thwaites, *Original Journals*; see, for example, 2: 15, 34–37, 187, 261, 270; 4: 294, 314, 319; 5: 48, 56, 67, 86, 115, 276, 278–80, 342.   [7]Coues, *Meriwether Lewis and William Clark*, 648.

The View from the Back

By late March the men were eager to be off, but they were delayed until April 7 by the late breakup of ice on the river after the unusually cold winter. While waiting, they put the finishing touches on the canoes and amused themselves watching the Indians jumping from floe to floe as they snared the carcasses of buffaloes drowned in the breakup.[8] At last, the floes dwindled and the river was high enough for the men to load the eight vessels: two pirogues, each with a mast and sail, and six canoes.[9] Now they were ready to follow the river off the end of the map.

During the journey, Jean-Baptiste was mostly immobile in his cradleboard, sling, or bier, but he could move his head freely.[10] Aboard the white pirogue, he had plenty of stimulating sights, sounds, and smells to enjoy as he watched the world pass by from his mother's back. He could see the sail rippling in the wind and watch eagles fishing and flocks of swans and geese flying north as the pirogue fought its way west against the current. The lively tunes and banter of the pirogue's six oarsmen filled his ears as he watched the larger red pirogue, the six cottonwood canoes, and the last of the ice floes bob along in the fast waters. The scent and smoke of

---

[8] Moulton, *Journals* 3: March 29, 1805.
[9] Verne Huser ("On the Rivers with Lewis and Clark," 17–24) describes the white pirogue as about thirty-five feet long and five feet wide at the bow, with a mast, sail, tiller, and rudder. It had six rowing positions and an eight-ton capacity. The red pirogue was a little larger, with seven rowing positions and a nine-ton capacity. Although the canoes were smaller, they were not lightweight—imagine portaging six cottonwood canoes weighing about three thousand pounds each.
[10] Hunsaker, *Sacagawea Speaks*, 125, n.33. In the Lewis and Clark Journals, Jean-Baptiste is carried in a "bier." Joseph Mussulman ("Pomp's bier was a bar") argues that Jean-Baptiste's bier was a mosquito bar or net. He adds that the Lemhi Shoshoni hold that Sacagawea would have carried her baby in a cradleboard, while the Hidatsa say she would have wrapped him in a shawl or blanket draped over her shoulder. According to W. Dale Nelson (*Interpreters with Lewis and Clark: The Story of Sacagawea and Toussaint Charbonneau*, 28), Jean-Baptiste was carried in a basket-like cradle made of cord that the captains had brought with them.

burning vegetation wafted over the river to him from fields, burnt each spring before planting. From time to time his mother would shift him forward to suckle or freshen his coverings or just play and coo with him. Then, in the evenings, he was put to sleep alongside his parents in the same skin-dressed tent as Lewis, Clark, and Drouillard, his mother calming him so his cries would not disturb the exhausted men.

Fortunately, he was too young to sense the danger when, just six days along, and again on May 10, the pirogue carrying him and his parents was nearly upset. But even the baby could not escape the discomfort everyone endured a few days later when the wind blasted their faces with fine sand, stinging everyone's eyes.[11] Yet something much more ominous lay ahead. By mid-June, Sacagawea came down with what would prove to be a very dangerous illness. As her condition worsened, the men worried not only for her life, but for her baby's as well. At four months old, he could not possibly survive on this wild river trail without a woman's milk. Yet the young mother somehow managed to continue to nurse her baby through the several days she lay gravely ill. By June 16, however, she was so ill that she refused essential medicines and mineral waters offered by the captains. It was only at Toussaint's insistence that she took them.[12] Fortunately, she did not have to be moved from her sick bed; the journey had ground to a halt as the captains studied the portage of the Great Falls. With time, worry was lifted and joy returned to camp as her recovery progressed. Jean-Baptiste must have delighted at the happy sound of Cruzatte's fiddle on June 25 and the hilarious sight of the men jumping up and down as they danced around the campfire. He could also enjoy famil-

---

[11] Coues, *Meriwether Lewis and William Clark*, 269–70, 280, 310.
[12] Nelson, *Interpreters with Lewis and Clark*, 31.

iar aromas in the warm night air as his father made his camp specialties, which were such great favorites with the men.[13]

Barely well again, Sacagawea, along with Toussaint and Jean-Baptiste, soon embarked on another potentially disastrous adventure, when, on June 29, they accompanied Clark and York to see a waterfall. As it started to rain, they took refuge in a ravine, not realizing the danger that flash floods pose in the West. As the rain increased, suddenly a great torrent of water rolled toward them full of mud, rocks, and debris. Clark had only seconds to react. Securing his gun and shot-pouch in his left hand, he used his right to push Sacagawea, with Jean-Baptiste in her arms, up the steep bluff ahead of him. Meanwhile, Toussaint who was uphill, frantically pulled his wife and son up from above. So quickly had this mad scramble begun that Clark had lost his compass and umbrella, and Charbonneau his gun, shot-pouch, and tomahawk. Sacagawea had just managed to snatch Jean-Baptiste naked from his bier as it and his clothes were swept away by the torrent. All of them would have been washed over the falls had it not been for the swift reactions of Clark and Toussaint.[14]

Having abandoned the pirogues at the Great Falls, now Sacagawea either walked along the shore with her son or rode in one of the canoes. More dangers awaited. As they approached Shoshoni territory, Sacagawea and Jean-Baptiste nearly missed their happy reunion with their relatives when rattlesnakes threatened both the Indian woman and Clark as they walked along the riverbank.[15] But two days later, on August 17, the joyful encounter did at last take place. The Charbonneau family was walking beside the river, about a hundred yards ahead of the party, when both Toussaint and

---

[13]Coues, *Meriwether Lewis and William Clark*, 376–77, 390.
[14]Ibid., 394–95.   [15]Ibid., 502.

Sacagawea coins.
United States Mint image.

the usually reticent Sacagawea suddenly began "to dance and show every mark of the most extravagant joy."[16] She had recognized her people approaching them on horseback! Using Plains Indian sign language signaling "this is my people," she sucked her fingers, as a child suckles nourishment from its mother. The Indians, too, "sang aloud with the greatest appearance of delight."[17] But the best was yet to come— many emotional reunions with old friends and relatives not seen for five years. How relieved she was to see among them a dear friend who had been taken with her in the raid but who had somehow managed to escape and find her way safe-

---

[16] Ibid., 509.   [17] Ibid.

ly home. Imagine Sacagawea's pride as she showed her handsome six-month-old son to this brave friend and her whole tribe, and especially to his uncle, tribal chief Cameahwait. Yes, in an amazing turn of events, she had recognized her brother as she had begun to translate for the Corps. She had to contain her excitement as she listened carefully to her brother's words, which she had to render into Hidatsa for Toussaint, who then gave the French version to Labiche for translation into English for Lewis and Clark. As the Hidatsa words left her tongue, the brother and sister had a few quiet moments to gaze at one another and recall their carefree childhood days together at that spot. This happy sojourn was also Jean-Baptiste's first chance to see other babies and children, including his orphaned cousin, the son of Sacagawea's sister. So far, he had lived entirely among thirty-one grown men and his mother. Now he was the center of attention for a multitude of excited women and children.

Had Sacagawea pressed a case for remaining with her people to care for her orphaned nephew or to honor a commitment made in childhood to marry a certain tribesman, it seems likely Lewis and Clark would have acquiesced to her wishes. She had fulfilled her obligation to them by securing about thirty horses from her tribe and she was now less essential. At the very least, they would have agreed to leave her there on the return trip. If she had been married off to Toussaint against her will and if he were indeed the abusive tyrant described by Coues,[18] she would have been encouraged to leave him. The captains would have been relieved to have Jean-Baptiste "liberated" from a future under the brutal hand of his father. There is no mention, however, that Sacagawea ever considered such an option. She chose to continue on to the coast with her husband, baby, and the Corps of Discovery.

---
[18]See Chapter One, n.22 and 23.

She may have questioned this decision in the next few weeks as her emotions were dampened by cold and hunger. The gap on the map had proved much more arduous and lengthy a mountain trek than any of them had foreseen. Near starvation in the Bitterroots, somehow this teenaged girl managed to keep her baby dry, nourished, and healthy. At last, they emerged from the last range of mountains and could rest and recover with the help of the Nez Perce, as the men constructed six new canoes from ponderosa pine.[19] Then, as Captain Clark and the Charbonneaus walked along the Columbia River, Jean-Baptiste could share their first view of Mt. Hood, long anxiously anticipated from Broughton's 1792 map.[20] At last, they were back in their known world, and the captains realized that soon the ocean would be in view. But first, they had to safely cross the open territories of unknown tribes. Jean-Baptiste's presence and that of his mother greatly reduced the danger, reassuring the Columbia River tribes that this was indeed a peaceful mission. It was unthinkable to them that warriors would bring a woman and a baby on a raid.[21]

What a triumph when they finally reached their goal in late November! In the first vote ever cast by a woman in (what soon would be) all of America, Sacagawea confidently weighed in with her opinion as to where they should build their winter quarters. Well aware of the many times that roots gathered by the women had saved her tribe after animal resources had failed to materialize, she voted for a place

---

[19] Verne Huser ("On the Rivers with Lewis and Clark," 17–24) describes the various vessels used by the Corps. The Nez Perce taught them how to burn out ponderosa pine logs to save themselves the work of hollowing them by ax.

[20] In 1792, Lieutenant William Broughton, on orders from Captain George Vancouver of England, led the first exploratory expedition up the Columbia River by non-natives. He proceeded about as far as the Sandy River, just east of present-day Portland, Oregon (Washougal on the Washington side). His maps were used thirteen years later by Lewis and Clark.

[21] Coues, *Meriwether Lewis and William Clark*, 646, 648.

where there were plenty of "Potas" (roots).[22] Their camp, however, was not in view of the ocean; instead it was in a sheltered wood. Dreary, wet day followed dreary, wet day, but Sacagawea's confident optimism did not falter, and when she had still not seen the Pacific by early January, she made it clear to Clark that she wanted to be included in the group going to the ocean to see a beached whale. Clark respected her wishes and agreed to include the Charbonneaus in the party. This jaunt lifted everyone's spirits, especially as "The weather was beautiful, the more agreeable as this is the first fair evening we have enjoyed for two months."[23] No one wrote about the reactions of Sacagawea and her eleven-month-old son upon seeing the boundless ocean for the first time. Perhaps she remained calm—she usually kept her feelings to herself—but her emotions must have been running high as she realized a dream she had envisioned for the fourteen months this goal had been on her mind.

Jean-Baptiste spent his first birthday in and around the quarters he shared with his parents within Fort Clatsop. He must have been fully ambulatory and beginning to talk by the time he settled onto his mother's back again on March 23, 1806, for the long march home.

Return Trip Home

Most everyone else had suffered numerous illnesses over the months, but Jean-Baptiste had remained remarkably healthy so far, a true testament to Sacagawea's mothering skills and a strong disposition. But that would change on the journey home. On May 22, 1806, Clark tells us, "Shabonos son a small child is dangerously ill. his jaw and throat is much swelled. we apply a poltice of onions, after

---

[22] Ambrose, *Undaunted Courage*, 311.
[23] Coues, *Meriwether Lewis and William Clark*, 745–46.

giveing him some creem of tarter &c." The next day, the baby seemed to be doing better: "the Creem of tartar and sulpher operated several times on the child in the course of the last night, he is considerably better this morning, tho' the swelling of the neck has abated but little; we still apply pol[t]ices of onions which we renew frequently in the course of the day and night."[24] It seems Lewis and Clark were up all night with the baby. Perhaps this is when the life-long bond between Clark and Jean-Baptiste was forged.

The optimism of May 23 was crushed a few hours later when "The child was very wrestles last night; it's jaw and the back of it's neck are much more swollen than they were yesterday tho' his fever has abated considerably. We gave it a doze of creem of tartar and applied a fresh poltice of onions."[25] Then, Jean-Baptiste had yet another bad night and a worried Lewis reported on the rainy morning of May 25 that "the Child is more unwell than yesterday."[26] At some point, a new patient, an old Indian chief, had been brought to them and the two captains labored over him, as well as the little boy, for many long days and nights until finally, by June 8, both were nearly well again. A modern-day doctor, E. G. Chuinard, believes Jean-Baptiste suffered from an external abscess on the side of his neck or mastoiditis and was near death; it was "good doctoring, good mother's care, and good luck saved this little fellow for an interesting saga all his own."[27]

The journey rolled on all that summer with the Charbonneaus continuing to ably assist the expedition and with little Jean-Baptiste becoming even more endearing as his personality developed. At some point that summer, he must have begun entertaining the Corps with his dancing since Clark later referred to him as his "little dancing boy."[28] Perhaps he

---

[24]Thwaites, *Original Journals*, 5: 57–58. [25]Ibid., 5: 60. [26]Ibid., 5: 63.
[27]Chuinard, *Only One Man Died*, 370, 374.
[28]Thwaites, *Original Journals*, Appendix 59: 329–30.

danced around the campfire as Cruzatte played his lively tunes on the fiddle. At some point, Clark gave him the nickname "Pomp." Since the usual dictionary definition for "pomp" is "ostentatious display," some speculate that the lad was given this name for his extravagant dancing style. It is easy to imagine a proudly strutting little tyke bringing a crowd of grown men to tears as they clapped and laughed. Or perhaps he was named for the great Roman general and statesman, Pompey.[29] This seems quite plausible, considering that seventeen-month-old Jean-Baptiste was honored that summer with his own landmark, "Pompy's Tower," a massive land formation on the Yellowstone River. Clark carved his own name into the stone monolith July 25, 1806, where it remains visible to this day. Now called "Pompeys Pillar," President Clinton declared it a national monument on January 17, 2001. Nearby "Baptiste's Creek" may have been named for Jean-Baptiste as well.[30]

By August, all were anxious to return home especially as the mosquito attacks worsened. Even Jean-Baptiste's little face was swollen from bites, having lost his mosquito-netted bier the summer before. Finally, on August 17, 1806, the villages of the Minnetarees (Hidatsa) came into view. Joyful greetings from thousands of villagers overwhelmed them;

---

[29] Although Helen A. Howard ("The Puzzle of Baptiste Charbonneau," 12), Speck (*Breeds and Half-Breeds*), Marion Tinling (*Sacagawea's Son*), and others repeat the notion that "Pomp" was a Shoshoni name given a firstborn son, linguists find no evidence for this. Anderson ("A Charbonneau Family Portrait," 5–6) cites personal communication with linguist Wick R. Miller, who believed that neither "Sacajawea" nor "Pomp" were Shoshoni words. Anderson and Schroer ("Sacagawea: Her Name and Destiny," 6) thought that Clark gave Jean-Baptiste this nickname for his dancing style. Since Clark named a landmark "Pompey's Tower" for the boy, I suggest Pomp was named for Pompey, the Roman general who erected Pompey's Pillar in Alexandria. Clark had his little joke here, comparing this "tower" of his little Pomp to the "pillar" of the great Roman general and statesman, Gnaeus Pompeius Magnus (Pompey). The National Monument committee chose a more serious interpretation, giving it the ancient name, "Pompey's Pillar," rather than the name Clark actually gave it, which was "Pompy's Tower."

[30] Thomasma, *The Truth about Sacajawea*, 84.

Pompey's Tower.
Courtesy Jim Wark.

there had been so many months of near isolation. It was time for the Charbonneaus to part from the Corps. Contrary to what is commonly believed, Lewis and Clark were not glad to see the last of Toussaint. Lewis' assessment was somewhat tepid, referring to Toussaint as "a man of no peculiar [particular] merit; [who] was useful as an interpreter only, in which capacity he discharged his duties with good faith, from the moment of our departure from the Mandans, on the 7th of April, 1805, until our return to that place in August last."[31] Clark, on the other hand, had a higher opinion of Toussaint's worth, and they went on to have a "sus-

---
[31]Jackson, *Letters of the Lewis and Clark Expedition*, 369.

tained, lifelong friendship."[32] Clark pressed him to return with him to St. Louis, but Toussaint made it clear that he did not wish to live among city folks. Clark's fondness for the family was apparent in his words of parting. He was very appreciative of their services and felt badly that Sacagawea had not been compensated for her good work. In truth, he had grown fond of all three of them, but he had grown especially close to Jean-Baptiste, whom he called a "butifull promising child."[33] In fact, he wanted to take Jean-Baptiste with him to St. Louis and raise him as his own. The parents realized what a wonderful opportunity this would be for their son, and they accepted Clark's offer, but they asked him to wait a year until the boy was weaned and able to get along without his mother.

Just three days later, on August 20, Clark wrote to Toussaint from the pirogue as he made his way back to St. Louis. Already he was missing little Pomp. He again urged Toussaint to come to St. Louis, and he renewed his offer to raise the boy:

> You have been a long time with me and have conducted your Self in Such a manner as to gain my friendship, your woman who accompanied you that long dangerous and fatigueing rout to the Pacific Ocean and back, diserved a greater reward for her attention and Services on that rout than we had in our power to give her at the Mandans. As to your little Son (my boy *Pomp*) you well know my fondneſs for him and my anxiety to take and raise him as my own child. I once more tell you if you bring your son Baptiest to me I will educate him and treat him as my own child. . . .
>
> Wishing you and your family great suckceſs & with anxious expectations of seeing my little dancing boy Baptiest, I shall remain your friend.
>
> William Clark[34]

---

[32] Anderson, "A Charbonneau Family Portrait," 13.
[33] Thwaites, *Original Journals*, 5: 344.   [34] Ibid., Appendix 59: 330.

This offer is extraordinary considering that Clark was a bachelor at the time and could not have been very certain about his own future. Would he be able to settle down in St. Louis and take full responsibility for a toddler, or would duty call him elsewhere? How well did he think through this offer? It seems this boy had touched his heart and, when it came time to say good-bye to him, Clark realized how much he had grown to love him. Twice in three days he had pressed his appeal on Toussaint for the lad. Clark was ready to become a family man, and it was with Jean-Baptiste that he wanted to begin that family. But perhaps there was more to it.

Jean-Baptiste's Jeffersonian Heritage

William Clark had brought the Jeffersonian intellectual worldview with him from Virginia. It was that unique worldview, and his obvious affection, that caused Clark to be so set on making farmers of Toussaint and Sacagawea and a scholar of Jean-Baptiste. In addition to the cultures of his mother and father, Jean-Baptiste would also adopt that of his Jeffersonian mentor, William Clark.

Thomas Jefferson and his fellow Virginians, Lewis and Clark, were men of the Enlightenment. This philosophy stressed the use of reason and science to understand how all life is related. Also important was the interrelationship of all the components of life, including both public and private interests, and intellectual and business pursuits. In other words, for them, the goal of a public servant was to seek harmony between all peoples, as well as between all the components of an individual's life. A man should pursue business interests as a public servant, always keeping in mind what is best for all those affected. The public good was seen as the core value.

Likewise, Jefferson believed that progress proceeds best when all aspire to unravel the secrets of the universe. This was why the scientific component of the Lewis and Clark Expedition was so essential. This component went hand-in-hand with the main component of the quest—that of seeking trade routes and relationships in order to enhance business opportunities. Jefferson felt he could best affect both trade development and the good of the people if he gathered as much information as possible about all resources, both human and environmental. He could then formulate a harmonious policy for the betterment of all.

This philosophy ties in with his view of the Indian. Jefferson and Clark were in agreement that Indians were not an inferior race. They were in every way capable of living as white men lived. As Jefferson saw it, they were currently living at a lower level of cultural attainment because of their environmental history. If they were set on the right path and were assisted in their progress down that path, they would soon embrace the harmony of the enlightened society. The main problem, in Jefferson's view, was that they had too much collective land. As long as they could get along by hunting and gathering, they would not become individual property owners and settled agriculturalists; and, therefore, they would not join in on the cultural benefits enjoyed by their propertied white neighbors. He felt it was in the Indians' best interests, therefore, to encourage them to give up their large tracts of land and their wandering ways. Then they would strive to fit in with the whites with whom they would share the territory. (Of course, those with less-pure motives would soon corrupt this philosophy to their own advantage, but there is every reason to believe, from the words and actions of Jefferson and Clark, that the above was their true motivation, ethnocentric but well-meaning.)

This vision of melding white men and Indians into a brave new agricultural society was a likely motivation behind Clark's encouragement of Toussaint to purchase land and settle down in St. Louis. Sacagawea's role was also important to the plan. She was admired by Indians, as well as by whites, for her role in the Corps of Discovery expedition; and her admiration for the ways of the whites surely delighted Clark. If she and her husband could settle down as farmers and raise a *métis* son who was a scholar and a community leader, Indians would be impressed and would emulate this precedent. This all-American family, which had been a part of the Corps of Discovery itself, would symbolize what the expedition was striving to attain. Clark's dream soon fell apart, however, when, after just five months, Toussaint and Sacagawea gave up their new life on the farm and decided to return to the West. But Jean-Baptiste remained. Perhaps he would become the example for his people that Clark sought in order to demonstrate the superiority of choosing the white culture over old Indian ways. Perhaps he would be the template for the citizen Indian.

It is often overlooked that Lewis, too, brought a *métis* child home to St. Louis. This was thirteen-year-old Toussaint Jessaume, son of René Jessaume, the fur-trader who delivered Jean-Baptiste. Clearly, Lewis and Clark wanted to demonstrate their accord with the missionaries that the education of the Indian was a necessity and a priority. Jeffersonians, like Lewis and Clark, were devoted to the concept that all men should be given the opportunity to develop their talents to the fullest. *Métis* boys like Jean-Baptiste Charbonneau and Toussaint Jessaume could lead the way, uniting their Indian and white relatives in a harmonious future. Wide-eyed Jean-Baptiste, innocent of these expectations, would soon enter the enlightened, optimistic town of St. Louis.

Hidatsa Boy

But first, Jean-Baptiste could enjoy some carefree formative years with his parents and the Hidatsa people of *Awatixa*, "the little village," on the Knife River. Although he would be just four years old on leaving this Indian village, the values learned there would be lasting. Studies have shown that

> The traditions, folkways, and mores of a society weave their subtle fabric around the infant from the moment of birth—and, indeed, even before birth: patterns of behavior in the broad society as well as in specific subcultural groups, impinge upon the infant and shape his deepest responses to the environment into which he is born.[35]

Upon returning to *Awatixa* that mid-August day of 1806, the family enjoyed their summer quarters for a while before retreating to their forest home for the winter. It was among the children of the forty lodges of this small village that Jean-Baptiste formed his first friendships, but he interacted with a much larger array of men, women, and children, as well, among the nearly four thousand total villagers in this confederation of Mandan and Hidatsa peoples. As a toddler, he accompanied his mother and the other women and children into the fields where they tended their crops. On special occasions, he followed her into the center of the village where the important events were held, like the summer Okipe ceremony. Here he watched and wondered as the warriors prayed, danced, and performed painful rituals to insure rejuvenation of the crops and the buffalo.

---

[35] Edith W. King and August Kerber, *The Sociology of Early Childhood Education*, 43. For the importance of the first five years on forming values also see, for example, C. H. Cooley, *Human Nature and the Social Order*; G. H. Mead, *Mind, Self and Society, From the Standpoint of a Social Behaviorist*, Part 3; Jean Piaget, *The Language and Thought of the Child*; Erik Erikson, *Childhood and Society*; Fred Greenstein, *Children and Politics*; David Easton and Robert Hess, "The Child's Political World"; and Yehudi Cohen, *Social Structure and Personality*.

Buffalo Bull Dance of the Mandan Indians.

Ptihn-Tak-Ochata, Dance of the Mandan.
Both illustrations by Karl Bodmer.
Courtesy the Library of Congress.

Each day, he and his fellow villagers bathed in the river, even in winter when they had to poke bathing holes into the ice. This would be good training for his future life in the wilderness, as was the busy life of the Hidatsa throughout the winter. These hardy people did not huddle in their lodges against the cold. They were out of doors most of the time, back and forth across river, which was often frozen for as long as four months at a time—from November to March. On this vast expanse of ice, Jean-Baptiste joined the other children in their games while Sacagawea transported goods from one side of the river to the other by sledge and his father sought thick winter pelts for trade.

Winter also presented Jean-Baptiste with a rich ceremonial life. Dances and chants, many to do with rites of passage, often invigorated the icy night air. The buffalo bull dance was particularly exciting, as the warriors in its society (the *Beróck-Óchatä*) donned the head, horns, and robe of the beast and imitated its movements as they danced. The eager eyes of Jean-Baptiste and the other children locked onto those of the two main dancers, peering out at them from the leather-rimmed eyeholes of their buffalo heads. These were the two bravest warriors, the ones who had pledged to doggedly hold one position in the hunt and not stray from it, either killing the buffalo or dying in the attempt.[36] This impression of ideal manhood was lodged in his subconscious and it would inform his own buffalo days to come. But those days were still far off. He would spend the next few years in the white culture of St. Louis and Europe before he could return to these roots.

---

[36]Schierle, ed. (*Travels in the Interior of North America*, 30–33), describes the aspects of Hidatsa and Mandan life portrayed in this section, which are based on Prince Maximilian's studies of 1832–34; Toussaint Charbonneau assisted the prince, interpreting the language and culture.

Chapter Three

The Charbonneaus in St. Louis

Many and powerful as were the attractions of the settlements, we looked back regretfully to the wildness behind us.
—*Francis Parkman, 1846*

Toussaint and Sacagawea must have been torn by the prospect of separating from their only child. Although Clark had hoped to get his Pomp in 1807, there is no record of the Charbonneau family actually arriving in St. Louis before the fall of 1809.[1] Arikara attacks had brought a halt to the fur trade for about two years, making it dangerous to travel the river until late September of that year, when protection could be provided by the Chouteau expedition. It is likely that the Charbonneaus waited for that opportunity. Toussaint had plenty of incentive for making the trip. Aside from his understanding with Clark as to Jean-Baptiste, there was also a bonus awaiting him. On March 3, 1807, Congress had approved an award of 320 acres and double pay to each of the men who had accompanied Lewis and Clark, including Toussaint Charbonneau.[2]

---
[1] The arrival may have been as late as December 1809 (Rogers, *Lewis and Clark in Missouri*, 111).
[2] Act of Congress dated March 3, 1807 (2 Stat. 65–66; Private Laws, Ninth Congress, 2nd Session): Chapter 32: An Act Making Compensation to Messrs. Lewis and Clarke [*sic*] and Their Companions. Also see Irving W. Anderson, "Probing the Riddle of the Bird Woman."

The first documentation of the family's presence in St. Louis is Jean-Baptiste's baptismal record, dated December 28, 1809. Although probably no longer a practicing Catholic, perhaps Toussaint had not completely forsaken the core beliefs of his youth in Boucherville. He certainly went through a lot of trouble to arrange this ceremony. With no priest in residence, a monk had to be brought from several miles away across the river in the dead of winter. Toussaint may only have wanted to safeguard his son's soul through baptism, believing this sacrament necessary to solemnize the transition from pagan to Christian—from "savage to civilized," as the Church put it. Perhaps, too, he was trying to safeguard Jean-Baptiste's earthly future as well, for he chose as the godparents Auguste Chouteau and his twelve-year-old daughter Eulalie.[3] As was the practice in Quebec, the head of the highest ranking family in town had been sought as the godfather, someone to whom a lad could turn to ensure his future. In Auguste Chouteau, Toussaint had scored a major coup, for this middle-aged gentleman was the very René Auguste Chouteau who, in 1764, as a lad of thirteen, had co-founded St. Louis with his step-father, Pierre Liguest Laclede. Even as a youth, Auguste had proven his worth in the fur trade. He and his brother, Pierre, had gone on to found a mercantile empire that would dominate the economic development of St. Louis for genera-

---

[3]Bob Moore ("Pompey's Baptism, A recently discovered document sheds light on the christening of Jean Baptiste Charbonneau," 11) provides the text of the baptismal record in the original French and with English translation. He discovered it in the Register of Baptisms of the Old Cathedral Parish. The full name of the godmother was Marie Thérèse Eulalie Chouteau, 1797–1835. William Clark and his wife and baby were not present at the baptism. Lewis's shocking death (just two months prior) had delayed the Clark family's return to St. Louis. Moore also points out that Toussaint must have made a special effort to ensure his son was baptized—not only securing the consent of Chouteau as godfather, but also finding a priest to officiate, since St. Louis had no resident priest at that time; thus, a monk had to be brought in.

tions to come, and the Chouteau family would remain its leading family for at least a century.[4]

With Auguste Chouteau as his godfather and William Clark as his guardian, young Jean-Baptiste was off to an excellent start in his new life. Now nearly five years old, he must have looked to his parents for reassurance as they entered St. Louis' lone church. How strange this ceremonial building, made of vertical logs, looked to him. Although just sixty by thirty feet, it must have seemed large and peculiar in shape. He was used to the round structures of his village, not the square and rectangular buildings of this strange place. There was also a striking contrast between the fancy, flamboyant clothing of Eulalie and Auguste and the simple attire of his fur-trader father and his Shoshoni mother (who was described in the Baptismal record as "*Sauvagesse de la nation des Serpents*"). The Trappist monk who baptized him, Father Urbain Guillet, was wearing yet another type of clothing, the plain white robe of his order, and saying strange prayers over him in an unknown language while pouring water over his head. A peculiar ordeal indeed, but surprises would prove unending in this to foreign place called St. Louis.

It was fortunate for the boy's adjustment that the Charbonneaus remained in the St. Louis area together for well over a year before Jean-Baptiste was left solely in Clark's care. The next document verifying Toussaint's presence in St. Louis, dated January 31, 1810, is a War Department journal entry stating that Toussaint had collected $136.33 as his bonus from the Lewis and Clark Expedition. Other records confirm frequent contacts between Toussaint and Clark from April 1810 until March 1811.[5] Toussaint probably

---
[4]Janet Lecompte, "Pierre Chouteau, Junior," 24.
[5]Anderson ("Probing the Riddle of the Bird Woman," 10) cites "Account books of the Office of the Accountant of the War Department Journal Washington D.C.," 8231, as to the entry on January 31, 1810.

helped with the editing of the journals while in St. Louis,[6] clarifying items for an editor for whom the West was a considerable mystery.

Toussaint and Sacagawea did entertain thoughts of settling down in St. Louis, as Clark had repeatedly urged; on October 30, 1810, Toussaint obtained riverfront property from Clark in nearby Ferdinand Township. Besides respecting Clark's advice, he knew the benefits of the settled, civilized life of a farmer since he had grown up on a farm in Boucherville, and he certainly knew how to make a successful enterprise of it. But, like his ancestors, he chafed at the thought of being domesticated, of losing the freedom he had known in the untamed West. As Stanley Vestal is said to have observed, "No man, even the most polished and civilized, who has once savored the sweet liberty of the plains and mountains, ever went back to the monotony of the settlements without regrets and everlasting determination to return."

Just five months after buying the land from Clark, Toussaint sold it back to him. He had arranged to join Manuel Lisa's fur trading expedition as an interpreter and trader for $250 a year, and he eagerly awaited the departure date of April 2, 1811.[7] He spent half of the $100 he got for the land that March on hard-tack biscuits, stocking up for this return to the West with Sacagawea. A fellow passenger, Henry Brackenridge, left us this telling comment about the voyage:

> We have on board a Frenchman named Charbonet, with his wife, an Indian woman of the Snake nation, both of whom accompanied Lewis and Clark to the Pacific, and were of great service. The woman, a good creature, of mild and gentle disposition, was greatly attached to the whites, whose manners and airs she tries to imitate; but she had become sickly and longed to revisit her native

---

[6]Historian Barbara J. Kubik, "Sacagawea," public lecture, Vancouver, Wash., January 24, 2002.
[7]H. P. Howard, *Sacagawea*, 156–58: L. R. Hafen, ed., *The Mountain Men and the Fur Trade of the Far West*, 9: 57.

country; her husband also, who had spent many years amongst the Indians, was become weary of a civilized life. So true, it is, that the attachment to the savage state, or the state of nature, (with which appellation it has commonly been dignified,) is much stronger than to that of civilization, its refinements, and its security.[8]

Toussaint and Sacagawea were in accord. Although they had tried, they could not embody Clark's vision. The fact that they did not reject it out of hand is evidenced by the commitment of their son to the dream. But for them it would not work. They longed to go west again—he for the freedom and she to try to restore her health among her own people. Or could it be that her symptoms alarmed her so that she wanted to see her people again for traditional medicines or to die among friends in case she failed to recover? We cannot say; but, in truth, time was running out for this "good creature." If she did fear for her future, it must have been a comfort to be able to leave Jean-Baptiste in good hands, knowing that Clark would keep his word and raise her son as though he were his own.[9]

There is no record of Jean-Baptiste's reaction that sunny second day of April 1811, as he looked out onto the Mississippi to watch his parents embark. No steamboats met his searching eyes; the sturdy keelboat was the river workhorse in those days before steam had been harnessed. Fortunately, the river was high that spring and able to float Manuel Lisa's small but heavy, well-built keelboat, carrying over twenty crew and passengers and twenty tons of cargo. All of the supplies needed for an entire year of trade had been stowed aboard—awls, axes, beads, blankets, combs, cotton clothes, kettles, items for

---

[8] Henry M. Brackenridge, *Views of Louisiana*, 202.
[9] H. A. Howard ("The Puzzle of Baptiste Charbonneau," 12) assumes Jean-Baptiste accompanied his parents on their 1812 trip, and possibly on the 1811 trip as well. Brackenridge's failure to mention him, however, points to the more likely scenario that he stayed with Clark in 1811. Likewise, Luttig does not mention him present at Fort Manuel with his parents on the 1812 trip.

firearms, vermilion, buttons, and whiskey. It would have been a sad parting for the three Charbonneaus, but the joy of seeing old Hidatsa friends upriver after over a year's separation must have been of some solace to the parents as they missed their only child. They would remain in these villages on the upper Missouri for a complete year as Toussaint resumed his fur-trading activities and Sacagawea recovered.

Adjusting to a New Life

Toussaint and Sacagawea had failed to adjust to settled life in St. Louis. Would their son be more successful? Fortunately, Jean-Baptiste had had that year and a half in St. Louis (from fall 1809 until spring 1811) with his parents before he had to try to cope without them. There was so much for him to grasp and adapt to—life was so different from the Hidatsa ways and language he was used to. During that brief time they lived together as a family in the city, he had needed his parents' encouragement and advice as he struggled with learning civilized ways—that is, how he was expected to behave in the polite society of Clark's St. Louis. In the Indian manner, he had probably been indulged by his mother and was not used to being disciplined. As Francis Parkman learned when he visited the tribes in the 1840s, this traditional upbringing "tends not a little to foster that wild idea of liberty and utter intolerance of restraint which lie at the foundation of Indian character."[10]

During the fifth year of his life, not only did Jean-Baptiste have to learn the self-discipline necessary for attending school, but also more English to fit into the Clark household and better French to fit into the schoolroom. He also had to get used to the shoes, clothing, and ways of the city,

---
[10]Parkman, *The Oregon Trail*, 197.

plus prepare to part from his parents, in addition to learning how to cope with identity issues as an untutored "half-breed" among the more refined, *bourgeois* gentlemen's sons with whom he would be schooled. And then, just after his sixth birthday, it was time to say good-bye. Did any of the three sense the sad truth that they would never again live together as a family? However, since experiences in one's first five years form a lasting impression on a child's values, a solid foundation had been established to see him through. Jean-Baptiste would always carry within him the love of freedom he had learned from his parents and the Mandan/Hidatsa people. He had left the culture of his birth behind, but it would always be with him.

Lewis and Clark had to adjust to their changed lives as well. The first Clark family home that Jean-Baptiste visited with his parents may have been the one selected by Meriwether Lewis in the spring of 1808 when the co-captains were planning their hopeful beginnings together in St. Louis. Lewis, unlucky in love, must have felt a twinge of jealousy when Clark wrote him jubilantly from Virginia of his engagement. "I have made an [*sic*] attacked most vigorously, we have come to terms,"[11] teased Clark about his amorous campaign. Still a bachelor at the age of thirty-six, Clark had been eager to settle down on his return to civilization. Julia (also called Judith) Hancock had been on his mind for some time; he named the Judith River for her in the spring of 1805. When he had last seen her, she had been just twelve years of age, but by his return to Virginia in November 1806, she had blossomed into a lovely young woman just celebrating her sixteenth birthday. He was proud to make her his bride on January 5, 1808.

---

[11]William Clark Kennerly and Elizabeth Russell, *Persimmon Hill*, 20.

When Lewis found the house, Clark was still in Virginia with his new bride. He wrote to Clark in high spirits about the fine house he had taken for them in St. Louis at the corner of South Main and Spruce streets. It had plenty of room for family, entourage, and slaves. Although Lewis hoped to live on with the newlyweds, he realized this might not work out, and he was prepared to live elsewhere, perhaps just boarding there. Apparently, he was right about three being a crowd. Soon Lewis moved out of Clark's house and in with Pierre Chouteau, but he did continue to eat meals with the Clarks for a while, joined in 1809 by young Toussaint Jessaume, his ward. Soon the Clark family moved a few blocks south to Main and Pine.[12] Unfortunately, before Jean-Baptiste could join the reunion of his captains, Captain Lewis, unsuccessful in adjusting to his new life, died at his own hand.

Not all adjustments after the return to St. Louis were cultural and personal. Nature brought some surprises as well. What a shock they all experienced on December 16, 1811, when the tremendous forces of the New Madrid earthquakes began to shake the earth in a way totally unknown before or since. Nerves were shattered for hundreds of miles around the southern Missouri town of New Madrid (about 150 miles south of St. Louis) when three massive temblors (deduced to have ranged from 8.0 to 8.8 on the Richter Scale), plus about two thousand smaller ones, kept the ground shaking for three months. It is hard to imagine the terror little Jean-Baptiste must have experienced without his mother's comfort. But the shaking finally did stop in the

---

[12]Ambrose (*Undaunted Courage*, 438) describes this house at Main and Spruce, rented by Lewis in 1808. William Clark Kennerly, a family cousin born in 1824, states the newlyweds returned to St. Louis in the spring of 1808 and stayed temporarily in Auguste Chouteau's big house at Main and Market. Later, they rented the house of Benito Vasquez at Main and Pine, and this is where Julia's children were born. In 1818, Clark built the house on the southeast corner of Main and Vine where he lived until his death. Kennerly and Russell, *Persimmon Hill*, 25, 35.

spring of 1812, and soon afterwards his father was back in St. Louis to sign up again with Manuel Lisa, now a major power in the fur trade, who was organizing another expedition.[13] There is no mention if Sacagawea was with Toussant this time, but it may well be that both parents visited their son then. Sacagawea was pregnant with her second child. Perhaps she shared the good news with Jean-Baptiste that when they met next, he would have a new brother or sister.[14]

St. Louis in 1811

William Clark's St. Louis, which also became Jean-Baptiste's new life in 1811, was nothing like the one we know today. Although it was just a small town of about 1,400 souls, it was far from sleepy. Bursting with energy and enterprise, the city boasted about a dozen mercantile establishments and another dozen distilleries with nine water mills, six sawmills, fifteen horse mills, and two shot towers.[15] The New Madrid temblors may have seemed like an omen, for St. Louis was on the brink of great social, economic, and political upheavals after its relatively calm first half-century. Its beginnings went back to 1763 when it was first settled by Pierre Laclede Liguest and Auguste Chouteau as a fur trading center and a haven for Frenchmen escaping English rule after losing the French and Indian Wars. By 1811, St. Louis was on the brink of leaving these French roots behind and becoming the gateway to the West for American settlers from the East.

---

[13] Drumm, *Journals of a Fur-Trading Expedition*.

[14] Sacagawea was indeed with this 1812 expedition, but whether she joined the entourage in St. Louis or when it stopped at the Mandan villages is not known. It seems the expedition of 1811 and that of 1812 are sometimes confused. There were most definitely two distinct expeditions from St. Louis by Lisa in the subsequent springs of 1811 and 1812. Brackenridge was on the 1811 voyage of one keelboat. In 1812, there were two keelboats.

[15] *Missouri Gazette*, January 16, 1811. The 1810 census reported 5,667 in and around St. Louis.

The St. Louis of 1811 must have made Toussaint feel like he was back in Montreal. The language, culture, and village life were very similar to the towns he had known back in old Quebec. St. Louis was described as "traditional, honest, punctilious, law-abiding," with folks who were "unselfish, hospitable and friendly" and who enjoyed their many fêtes.[16] The same could be said of Montreal. One difference that Toussaint would have noticed, however, was the relative secularity of St. Louis. Montreal had always been a religious center and remained true to its roots as a Catholic mission, while the state of Catholicism in St. Louis, due to a scarcity of resident pastors, had thoroughly depressed its bishop.[17] Like Montreal, however, St. Louis was well-situated to become a major hub of the fur trade, and both cities were focused on fur-related commercial pursuits. As the *voyageurs* embarked for the West by way of the St. Lawrence, so too did the men of St. Louis strike out on the Mississippi and the Missouri. St. Louis, situated on the west bank of the Mississippi River just eighteen miles below the mouth of the Missouri, was an ideal jumping off spot for all westward explorations and expeditions. By 1811, it had evolved into a cosmopolitan town full of rough and ready fur traders and Indians of many tribes—along with Frenchmen, Spaniards, European nobles, Anglo-Americans, freed slaves, soldiers, merchants, missionaries, and all manner of adventurers—fueling its prosperity as they outfitted themselves for their western adventures and returned with its bounty. This was the bustling capital of Upper Louisiana, and it was a stimulating environment for a small boy to learn about the ways of the world beyond the village of his birth.

---

[16]Hiram M. Chittenden, *History of the American Fur Trade of the Far West*, 107.
[17]William Barnaby Faherty, S.J. (*Dream by the River*, 15), on Bishop Flaget's April 1814 visit to the St. Louis area.

Momentous events in 1811, like the battle of Tippecanoe that November, were happening all around young Jean-Baptiste as well. At the conclusion of this battle, which put down the massive Indian rebellion under Tecumseh, Clark had called together the most important Indian chiefs to try to win them over to the American cause. He had persuaded the chiefs of the Great and Little Osages, the Sacs, Renards, Delawares, and Shawnees to come with him to Washington, D.C., not only to treat with the president but also to make peace among themselves. It was their trust in Clark and his true regard for the Indian people that brought success to this mission. Under Clark's able management, the transition from Spanish/French to American governance was relatively smooth, and relations between the Americans and the Indian nations were improving.

Jean-Baptiste's World

When Jean-Baptiste moved into the heart of St. Louis, there was much to catch his eye. Main Street alone would have offered enough to enthrall any lad, with about a dozen general stores for him to explore, as well as the homes of friends, like his godfather's big house at the corner of Main and Vine. The street life was amazing—from uncouth traders in buckskins and moccasins to fine ladies dressed in the latest styles from New Orleans and Paris. Just a block away was the great Mississippi River, racing through the narrows fronting the city. From the promontory on which the town was situated, Jean-Baptiste could look down on its rocky shores. Here he could watch the fur traders and Indians coming and going, and he could wonder about his parents' journeys and dream about his future.

On his way home, as he descended the promontory, he

Plan of St. Louis MO 1822

Population 5,000
0.74 Sq. Miles

MISSISSIPPI RIVER

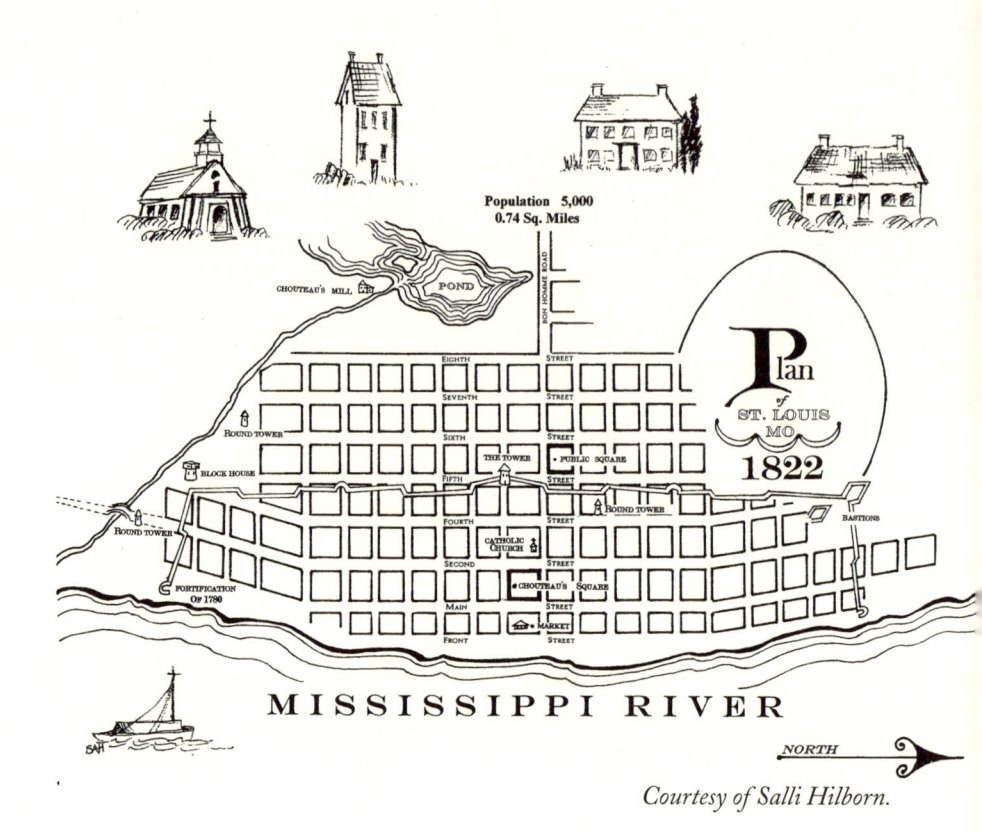

NORTH

Courtesy of Salli Hilborn.

could admire this St. Louis fanning out before him like an amphitheatre. Above the French-style *Place d'Armes*, he could see some fine houses of stone, as well as some wooden ones with the logs upright, as the French preferred, and generous porches below their steep roofs. The square, stone houses on quarter-block lots were whitewashed every year to turn a proud face to the river, like those of old Quebec on the St. Lawrence. He could also see the log church in which he had been baptized, built in 1776, as the Revolutionary War had raged in the East. And he could see the ribbons of farmland, just one acre wide but forty or fifty deep, rising from the river—a system first devised in seventeenth-century French Canada to give all farmers river access. Looking back to the center of town, he could admire some of the new public and commercial buildings—many quite fine—in various stages of construction, their roofs rising above the houses. Some housed new city services, like the *Missouri Republican*, its first newspaper, founded in 1808. Unlike his father, Jean-Baptiste would soon be able to read this paper on his own, allowing him to keep up on current events and thus participate in the world of ideas.

When Jean-Baptiste wandered just a few blocks in any direction, he could feel the burden of city life fall away as he stood before the open prairie, with its endless ripples of tall grass. A hike into the countryside would take him to the ruins of old stone forts built by the Spanish to hold off Indian attacks; if his rambles took him a short way to the northeast of town, he could see ancient Indian mounds, the most prominent of which were at Cahokia, just across the river (in present-day East St. Louis). Here had once stood the largest prehistoric complex north of Mexico, housing over 30,000 souls within its six square miles. Ironically, its grandest eminence, Monk's Mound, the largest prehistoric earthen construction in the New World, was now the home of the monk who had baptized Jean-Baptiste; the Trappists had chosen this imposing platform mound, over one hundred feet high, for their monastery. Much later, archaeologists would describe this complex as the largest community of the Mississippian culture. Its people had attained the highest level of cultural evolution in North America—not only geographically, but also in "extent of influence, ceremonialism, public works, technology, population density, and social stratification."[18] But this impressive civilization had disap-

---

[18] J. D. Jennings, *Prehistory of North America*, 246.

peared over four centuries before Jean-Baptiste's time. How he would have marveled to know that the Indian people had once built a city here far grander than this St. Louis. But all that was unknown then; the mounds were just a curiosity—promontories for monks' monasteries and for young boys to conquer. Soon much of it would be destroyed by the expansion of the city.

St. Louis and its surrounding countryside was a wonderful place for a small *métis* boy, not just physically, but also socially. Jean-Baptiste would not have been abused then because of his mix of white and Indian blood; intolerance would come later with the American expansion west. For now, little competition for resources and the need for trade by all sides meant tolerance. There was a notion of class, but it had to do with family connections rather than race, and Jean-Baptiste's connections to the Clark and Chouteau families were the best. The Indians of St. Louis felt right at home in those days prior to the War of 1812, and the French regularly intermarried with them. Although it was a frontier town, it was law-abiding. Leadership was sophisticated and well informed since, from its beginnings, St. Louis had had a great many highly literate men, educated in Canada and in Europe, to guide it.[19]

In sum, life in 1811 St. Louis was ideal for the Clark family, including Jean-Baptiste. After Manuel Lisa organized the Missouri Fur Company in 1808, a great industry had blossomed in which many would prosper, including the Clarks. William Clark's responsibilities grew with his mastery over the challenges presented by the acquisition of the Louisiana Territory. He was just the enlightened man for the delicate job of balancing the needs of the federal and local governments with Indian and commercial interests. He

---

[19]Faherty, *The Saint Louis Portrait*, 22, 29.

Monk's Mound, the largest prehistoric earthwork
in the Americas, is one hundred feet high over fourteen acres.
Courtesy Cahokia Mounds State Historic Site.

was fair-minded, respected by all parties, and perfectly suited to his responsibilities as principal Indian agent for the territory, which remained his position from 1807 to 1813. Jean-Baptiste thrived in his shadow.

1812 Brings Disasters

While 1811 was a year of promise for the Charbonneaus, 1812 brought great sorrows. By the end of that year, Sacagawea, just twenty-five years of age, would be no more. In May 1812, she had accompanied Toussaint and the Lisa party of eighty-five others to a site on the Missouri River in present-day South Dakota, just south of its border with

North Dakota, but the new Fort Manuel would not be ready for occupation until November 19. Questions remain as to the circumstances of Sacagawea's death: Did the Dakota winter and inadequate protection from the elements contribute to her precarious health, weakened from giving birth? Did she have the help she needed to give birth safely and avoid postpartum infections? Was she stricken by the same illness four months after this birth that she had endured four months after the birth of Jean-Baptiste?[20] Finally, Thomasma poses the sad question, "If Captain Lewis had been in Fort Manuel in December 1812, could he have once more saved the young Shoshoni mother?"[21]

The raging War of 1812, with the British agitating the Indians against the Americans, may have contributed to her illness as well. Fort Manuel was often in a state of confusion as various parties of warriors (some friendly, some not), traders, trappers, and travelers passed through that late summer and fall.[22] Toussaint's life was often in danger. John Luttig, Fort Manuel's clerk, recorded how Toussaint rode into the fort at full speed on September 17, 1812, announcing, "To arms, Lecomte is killed." Luttig's saddest entry, however was on December 20, 1812: "This evening the wife of Charbonneau, a Snake squaw, died of a putrid fever. She was a good and the best woman in the fort, aged about 25 years. She left a fine infant girl."[23]

This infant girl was Jean-Baptiste's sister, Lizette Charbonneau. Fortunately, Lizette still had her father with her,

---

[20]Dr. Chuinard (*Only One Man Died*, 287–89) deduces a possible diagnosis of chronic pelvic inflammatory disease from gonorrheal infection. It is also possible that Lizette was not born until December and that Sacagawea died of a postpartum infection. The supposition that the birth took place around August 1812 is based on the August 1813 guardianship proceedings, where Lizette is said to be about one year old.

[21]Thomasma, *The Truth About Sacajawea*, 92.

[22]Drumm, *Journal of a Fur-Trading Expedition*, 78–106; H. P. Howard, *Sacajawea*, 159–60.

[23]Drumm, *Journal of a Fur-Trading Expedition*, 106. One guess as to where Lizette got her name is the old voyageur song, "La Belle Lisette."

and it was he, most likely, who arranged for her care and wet nurse. Just one week later, Toussaint had to leave the fort for two months to work among the tribes, which was extremely dangerous. As he was returning to the fort on February 21, 1813, the Cheyennes warned him of imminent danger to his life; the very next day, another Frenchman was killed just outside the fort's walls. Toussaint saw hundreds of hostile Indians massing across the river, and he was very much aware of growing British influence among the Gros Ventres. Although he kept his boss fully apprised of these ominous developments,[24] Luttig chose to blame the messenger. He complained that Charbonneau and Jessaume "keep us in constant uproar with their histories and wish to make fear among the engagés."[25] But Toussaint's warnings proved well-founded. Had Luttig listened to him and evacuated sooner, there may have been less loss of life at the fort.

Again proving himself other than the worthless coward portrayed by Coues, "Toussaint served the American cause well by keeping the friendship of the Missouri Indians from swinging to the British."[26] It was Toussaint who was sent to the Rees (Arikaras) in November to try to make peace, and on March 1, even as the danger escalated, Toussaint agreed to go again to the Gros Ventre. This was just three days after Luttig recorded that all in the fort were "like Prisoners in Deserts to expect every moment our fate." Luttig was particularly nervous because very few men remained within the fort to defend it. Fifteen had been killed and many more had been taken prisoner; others were off trading and trapping.[27] Most of those left inside the fort were women and children, including Lizette. A few days after Toussaint's departure,

---

[24] Richard E. Oglesby, *Manuel Lisa and the Opening of the Missouri Fur Trade*, 140.
[25] Drumm, *Journal of a Fur-Trading Expedition*, 84, Luttig's journal entry Oct. 9, 1812.
[26] Hoffhaus, "French Made Lewis and Clark Expedition Successful."
[27] Drumm, *Journal of a Fur-Trading Expedition*, 140; Rogers, *Lewis and Clark in Missouri*, 112.

Luttig decided to make a desperate run for it. He and some of the others were successful, but many were lost, and soon Fort Manuel was burned to the ground.

As little Pomp had touched the heart of William Clark, so did baby Lizette arouse John Luttig's sympathies. It is apparent from his writings that Luttig admired Sacagawea a great deal; perhaps it was this regard that endeared him to her child. Before she died, Sacagawea may have appealed to him to take her infant daughter under his protection, or perhaps Toussaint had elicited a promise from him to protect Lizette if Toussaint did not return from his mission. In any case, John Luttig did not hand Lizette off to the Indian women. Rather, he took responsibility for her himself after making it back safely to St. Louis with her that June. Luttig assumed that Toussaint was dead and that Lizette was an orphan when he applied to the St. Louis courts that August 11, 1813, to be appointed her guardian. In the documents Lizette was described as "a girl about one year old." At the same time, he also applied for guardianship of "Toussaint, a boy about ten years old."[28] Although some argue that this Toussaint was Toussaint Charbonneau's son by his other Shoshoni wife, most historians now believe that this child was actually 8½-year-old Jean-Baptiste.[29]

If this boy was indeed Jean-Baptiste, then this court action raises many questions. Had Sacagawea and/or Toussaint asked Luttig to keep their son and daughter together? Why else would Luttig have also applied for Jean-Baptiste's guardianship in addition to Lizette's? Perhaps Luttig saw it as his duty to raise the children of a fallen employee. But he should have known that the boy was under Clark's care

---

[28]H. P. Howard, *Sacajawea*, 161.
[29]Ibid., 161–162, 170; Rogers, *Lewis and Clark in Missouri*, 113. This Toussaint could not have been Toussaint Jessaume, as he was seventeen years old in 1813, certainly too mature to be described as an ten-year-old boy.

since, by 1812, Clark had obtained documents from Toussaint Charbonneau entrusting Jean-Baptiste to his care while the boy attended boarding school. Drumm suggests that Luttig proceeded without input from Clark because Clark was not in St. Louis at the time.[30] In any case, Luttig's health was poor and two years later he passed away. By then, his name had been crossed out on the court documents and William Clark's had been entered.

Jean-Baptiste's New Family

During that terrible summer of 1813 and for some time afterwards, Jean-Baptiste believed he was an orphan. How relieved he must have been to finally see his father again three years later. We do not know for certain where he had been, but some say that Toussaint had been taken prisoner by the British in 1813 and again by the Spanish in 1815 (the latter occasion while on a trading expedition to the Southwest).[31] In any case, Toussaint was not seen again in St. Louis until 1816, when once again he signed up for a fur-trading expedition. This time he would accompany Julius McMunn to the upper Arkansas River. This contract covered July 1816 to July 1817, and his boss was again the trading mogul, Auguste Chouteau.[32] When father and son met again for this reunion, it may have been for the last time until Jean-Baptiste was a teenager.[33] William Clark had

---

[30]Drumm, *Journal of a Fur-Trading Expedition*, 133 and Introduction. Luttig, who had a drinking problem, died July 19, 1815.

[31]For example, see Ottoson ("Toussaint Charbonneau, A Most Durable Man," 152–85) as to 1813, and Hunsaker (*Sacagawea Speaks*, 88) and L. R. Hafen, ed. (*The Mountain Men and the Fur Trade of the Far West*, 9: 59) as to 1815. L. R. Hafen assumes Toussaint was with fellow traders imprisoned (some in irons) for forty-eight days by the Spaniards; but Nelson (*Interpreters with Lewis and Clark*, 75) doubts that Toussaint was imprisoned in Santa Fe.

[32]H. P. Howard, *Sacajawea*, 161.

[33]James W. Schultz (*Bird Woman*, 111–14) presents a story, told by Hugh Monroe, of Toussaint gambling away Jean-Baptiste's horse among the Mandan when the boy was eleven years old, but there are so many inconsistencies in these Schultz/Monroe tales that this cannot be taken seriously without further corroboration.

taken Toussaint's place as Jean-Baptiste's protector, and the young student was now immersed in the life of a St. Louis schoolboy.

Clark's family was now his family too, but perhaps Jean-Baptiste also had his own little sister Lizette waiting for him when he was home from school. Although references to her are nearly non-existent, we know that Clark did become her guardian in 1813 when she was about one year old. Since she was so young, she may have been placed elsewhere with a wet nurse. In any case, it is doubtful she was in Clark's home for her third birthday, since on August 8, 1814, all the children in the house were baptized by Bishop Flaget, but there was no mention of Lizette.[34] Indeed, Lizette then drops from our view forever, unless she is the "Elizabeth Carboneau" referred to nearly thirty years later as the mother of a baby girl. These records show that a Victoire, the daughter of Joseph Vertifeuille and Elizabeth Carboneau, was baptized at Westport, Missouri on April 23, 1843.[35] But this entry has not been definitely linked to our Lizette, who continues to be lost to history.

Besides Lizette, Jean-Baptiste may have shared his new world with another child of similar heritage and cultural background. This was Toussaint Jessaume, whose mother was an old friend of Sacagawea and whose father was Toussaint Charbonneau's friend, René Jessaume, the interpreter who assisted in Jean-Baptiste's birth and was also at Fort Manuel with Toussaint. Toussaint Jessaume, at the age of thirteen, had joined Meriwether Lewis in St. Louis in 1809, when he was indentured to Lewis for his care and educa-

---

[34] Bishop Flaget's journal cited by Faherty, *Dream by the River*, 15; copies of the baptismal records from the Cathedral of St. Louis for August 8, 1814, are in the possession of the author.   [35] H. P. Howard, *Sacajawea*, 162.

tion.[36] Perhaps this is the Toussaint others have assumed was a son of Toussaint Charbonneau. Research, however, has failed to verify any children for Toussaint Charbonneau besides Jean-Baptiste and Lizette, although he may well have had a child much later who died in the smallpox epidemic of 1837.[37]

The growing Clark family was also a part of Jean-Baptiste's life. By the time he was put into Clark's sole care in the spring of 1811, the Clarks had probably moved into their much-loved home at Main and Pine. It was here that Julia Clark's piano, shipped with much difficulty from the East, was proudly displayed. Aside from Jean-Baptiste, the happy couple had already produced one son of their own, and Julia was pregnant with another. After the firstborn, Meriwether Lewis Clark, arrived on January 10, 1809, the new father had given the teenaged mother a gift of the works of Shakespeare—a gesture consistent with his Jeffersonian philosophy of encouraging everyone, including women and Indians, to enter into the world of knowledge and ideas.[38] What a blow it must have been to this optimistic new family man to learn of the tragic suicide of his dear partner—Lewis had died just nine months after the birth of his namesake. At least, it was an eventual consolation to Clark that this namesake grew up to become a credit to the name. Good-looking, red-headed, and a civil engineer by age twenty-four, Meriwether Lewis Clark went on to serve in the Missouri House of Representatives and as recorder for the city of St. Louis. He was also the United States surveyor-general for the state

---

[36] A copy of this contract, dated May 13, 1809, is in the Grace Lewis Miller Papers, National Park Service, Jefferson National Expansion Memorial Archives, St. Louis. It is unknown if Toussaint Jessaume stayed on in St. Louis after Lewis' tragic death four months later. [37] Drumm, *Journal of a Fur-Trading Expedition*, 140.
[38] Ambrose, *Undaunted Courage*, 450.

of Missouri and a major in the Missouri battalion of artillery in the Mexican War, ending his distinguished career fighting on the Confederate side of the Civil War.

The second son, William Preston Clark, was born in October 1811, six months after the departure of Jean-Baptiste's parents. When Lizette Charbonneau became his ward in the summer of 1813, Clark had just been appointed governor of the Missouri Territory and Julia was expecting Mary Margaret. It must have been a heavy burden for this young woman to mother five children under the age of eight when she was just twenty-two years old herself. Besides her anxieties over the children, Julia Clark was also unnerved about the raging war. Writing to her brother shortly after Mary Margaret's birth, she concluded, "God only knows what our fate is to be."[39]

Schooldays in St. Louis

Perhaps Lizette was staying with a wet nurse during these difficult times and Jean-Baptiste was immersed in his education. He had not, however, been sent to a local public school, as there were no public schools in St. Louis until 1838. Before that, education was provided by tutors or in Catholic private schools. The first of these private schools was established in 1808 in nearby Genevieve by James Maxwell, a Spanish-educated Irish priest, but, with his death in 1814, that school had failed.

With his strong belief in the importance of education for both white and Indian children, Governor Clark, as chairman of the first school board of trustees, encouraged other Catholic religious, both priests and nuns, to fill this vacuum. Those answering the call included Philippine Duchesne,

---

[39]Julia Hancock Clark to George Hancock, Feb. 27, 1814, William Clark papers, Missouri Historical Society, Jefferson Memorial.

Pierre Jean De Smet, Joseph Rosati, and Louis W. V. Du Bourg, the latter two of which were also bishops of the Louisiana Territory. Most likely Jean-Baptiste was tutored for his first few years in St. Louis or sent to a small private school until 1818 brought the much-welcomed establishment of Bishop Du Bourg's St. Louis Academy.

Bishop Du Bourg, who had pursued advanced studies at the Sorbonne, was one of the best-educated men in America. He had come to St. Louis after serving as president of Georgetown College when the nation was so young that he had dined with President Washington at Mount Vernon. Although he was establishing a Catholic institution, he did not demand religious conformity, nor did he discriminate. Like St. Mary's College of Baltimore, which he had founded in 1805, his academy in St. Louis would be open to all creeds and nationalities. This modern attitude must have appealed to other enlightened men like William Clark who, though Episcopalian, encouraged his efforts.[40] Indeed, Clark was instrumental in helping fund Bishop Du Bourg's two-story brick academy, which had an associated seminary and church. It was just what he needed for his own sons and Jean-Baptiste, and it was just a few short blocks away (on the southwest corner of Second and Market), close to the Clark house at Main and Vine. Here, for twelve dollars a quarter, each of the boys could get a firm grounding in Greek, Latin, English, French, Spanish, and Italian, as well as arithmetic, mathematics, drawing, and geography. Boarding was available by mid-December 1819.

And so, Jean-Baptiste Charbonneau, then thirteen years old, began his formal studies at St. Louis Academy. Bishop Du Bourg may have taken a special interest in him since the

---

[40]Faherty, *Dream by the River*, 14–23.

good cleric shared Rousseau's romantic notions of "the noble savage" and was particularly interested in working with the Indians. At its inception, classes were conducted in French, but as the 1820s progressed and more Americans arrived, the shift was made to English. The new school, administered by Father François Niel, suffered a setback in the fall of 1820 with the death of its most prominent professor, Felix De Andreis, but his work was ably carried on by four other priests and four laymen. With a student body of just sixty-five boys, this was a ratio of one teacher to every eight students. Jean-Baptiste must have had a very good education indeed at this forerunner to present-day St. Louis University, which to this day proudly claims him as an alumnus.[41]

Unfortunately, Jean-Baptiste's school records have not survived, but it is doubtful that Clark would have wasted his time and money on him if he were not willing and able to profit from his studies. Clark's records for expenditures, beginning January 1, 1820, show tuition and room and board payments for "J. B. Charbonneau" to a Reverend J. E. Welch, a Baptist minister who boarded Indian and half-Indian boys. That May, tutoring payments went to a Reverend "Francis Neil" (the François Niel mentioned above, administrator of St. Louis Academy), for "Toussaint Charbonneau Jr.," a "half-Indian boy."[42] Clark allocated additional sums for school and personal supplies and services including: "one Roman history, Scott's Lessons, one dictionary, slate and pencils, paper and quills."[43]

---

[41]Jacques Vaillancourt, "Sacagawea 1790–1812," 39.

[42]H. P. Howard (*Sacajawea*, 170) says the payments were for "J.B. Charbonneau" and "Toussaint Charbonneau," but that they were "almost without doubt" the same boy. These data are from *American State Papers 1820*, Missouri Historical Society, St. Louis. Also see H. A. Howard, "The Puzzle of Baptiste Charbonneau," 12, and Drumm, *Journal of a Fur-Trading Expedition*, Appendix: 134. Nelson (*Interpreters with Lewis and Clark*, 76) adds payments to L. T. Honoré for boarding, lodging, and washing made March 31, June 30, and October 1, 1820.

[43]Drumm, *Journal of a Fur-Trading Expedition*, Appendix: 134.

Changing Times

The War of 1812 was a turning point for St. Louis. A great hatred for all Indians was growing in the wake of atrocities committed on homesteaders by British-allied Indians. Clark's philosophies were at odds with the mindset of the new settlers from the East to whom the idea of individual freedom and every man for himself superceded the concept of acting for the common good. Ironically, both sides agreed on the policy of Indian removal, although for totally different reasons and to be effected in totally different ways. Rather than assisting Indians to move west gradually in family groups and helping them to set up farms there, as Jefferson and Clark had envisioned, the prevailing attitude now was to eliminate them altogether or to move them all west as soon as possible in order to make the territory safe for the new American settlers. Old French customs were replaced by progressive East Coast imperatives. Merchants, too, grew impatient with the old ways; they were desperate to renew the prosperity lost in the war years. One of them, Christian Wilt, expressed a common sentiment when he wrote a friend recommending "slaying every Indian from here to the Rocky Mountains."[44]

As rapid growth from the East followed the War of 1812, the return to prosperity secured the progressive path and brought a rapid end to the old order. By 1816, the population of St. Louis had more than doubled from five years earlier, and the city limits had spread as well. By 1818, growth had brought the return of full prosperity. There were forty retail stores, a post office, a federal land office, two banks, a courthouse, a theatre, three churches, and a museum. The citizens

---
[44]Letter of August 6, 1814, from Christian Wilt to Joseph Herzog in "Letter Books of Christian Wilt," Letter No. 125, Missouri Historical Society, Jefferson Memorial. Ironically, it was in the very year of Clark's death (1838), that over fourteen thousand Cherokees were forced West in the Trail of Tears.

of St. Louis were said to be "beyond doubt the most happy and contented people whoever lived."[45] Fiddle music could be heard emanating from most homes in the evenings accompanying the nightly dances. In their revelry, the citizens would gravitate to Main Street where the well-to-do (like the Clark and Chouteau families) lived, in order to enjoy their generosity and hospitality. In 1816, the Clark family celebrated this return to prosperity by building a grand, two-story brick house on the southeast corner of Main and Vine. This would be Clark's home for the rest of his life. In its great council room, one hundred feet long by twenty-five feet wide and illuminated by massive chandeliers, Clark could at last fully display all his fine artifacts from his explorations and dealings with the tribes. Open to the public on request, this was the first museum west of the Mississippi. Many famous dignitaries, including Lafayette in 1825, marveled at the incomparable display of items, ranging from bear-claw necklaces to canoes to musical instruments.[46]

But, just as Clark was getting his bearings in this optimistic new environment, everything he had worked for, both personally and professionally, began to slip away. Julia's health failed. Even though Clark had been well situated as territorial governor of Missouri, and, one assumes, there had been ample staff to assist his young wife, perhaps giving birth to five children in eight years had taken too great a toll. The worried husband took her back to her former home in Fincastle, Virginia, hoping it would revitalize her, but, on June 27, 1820, Julia passed away at the age of twenty-eight. Sadly, six-year-old Mary Margaret, sent to live with Kentucky relatives, followed her the next year. And so, at the age

---
[45] Faherty, *The Saint Louis Portrait*, 45.
[46] Rogers, *Lewis and Clark in Missouri*, 122.

of fifteen, Jean-Baptiste had to suffer the loss of his second mother. Fortunately, the home was motherless for one year only. Clark found a new wife in Julia's first cousin, Harriet Kennerly Radford, who was also mourning the loss of a first spouse. She brought her own three children to the marriage, and she and Clark had two more together. But tragedy continued to befall the Clark home. A son, Edmond, died in 1827, and another son, John, plus Clark's second wife, Harriet, passed away in 1831. Devastated, Clark sent his youngest son, Jefferson Clark, just seven, to Harriet's sister to be raised.

Professional setbacks added to Clark's personal tragedies. He had become an anachronism. Jeffersonian values had been diminished by those of a new era in which individual goals replaced a focus on the community. These attitudes reflected changing ambitions—land fever, with the Indians seen as obstacles, had replaced fur fever, which valued Indians as trade partners. In old St. Louis, wealth and influence had been in the hands of the old-line, fur-focused French families like the Chouteaus, Gratiots, and Prattes, as well as those of sympathetic Americans, like Daniel Boone's son Nathan, Thomas Hart Benton, and Gov. William Clark. Gradually, however, in the decade that followed the war, political power and the will of the people had shifted. In this new age, Clark was perceived as too friendly with the Indian and not concerned enough about the settler (a charge that would later dog Jean-Baptiste, as well). Boone's Lick, the huge land grant just west of St. Louis (opened in 1819 by Nathan Boone) had attracted thousands, and these new settlers demanded security and policies that favored property holders. Clark was too preoccupied with Julia's failing health to launch an effective campaign addressing these concerns. All these political and personal problems came together to bring about Clark's failure in his bid for governor of the new state of Missouri in 1820. He was still respected in Washington, D.C., however, where his expertise in Indian affairs was recognized and remained unchallenged, and he was asked to stay on in St. Louis to manage Indian policy.

Over the years, Clark continued to call upon his faithful retainer, Toussaint Charbonneau, both as a fur trader for the Missouri Fur Company (in which Clark had major financial interests) and as an interpreter, guide, and diplomat. Toussaint's employment for the United States Indian Department, Upper Missouri sub-agency, for which he received the generous remuneration of four hundred dollars a year, lasted from 1819 until 1838. His many clients included Prince Maximilian of Wied, Duke Paul of Württemburg, Colonel Henry Leavenworth, General Henry Atkinson, Major Stephen J. Long, Karl Bodmer, George Catlin, William Sublette, Francis Chardon, Charles Larpenteur, and others.[47] No doubt Jean-Baptiste saw his father on some occasions when Toussaint reported to Clark for his assignments, and he may have accompanied him from time to time, but for the most part, the lad remained in St. Louis for his schooling.

There he continued to witness historic events. He must have been there, for example, on that unforgettable summer's day in 1817 when the whole town turned out to welcome the *Zebulon Pike*, the first steamboat to come as far north as St. Louis. Although relations had suffered following the War of 1812, whites and Indians still intermingled to some extent in St. Louis, and on that day they stood together on the banks of the Mississippi in great anticipation. At the first sight of the steaming monster, however, the Indians

---

[47] Anderson, "A Charbonneau Family Portrait," 13; L. R. Hafen, ed., *The Mountain Men and the Fur Trade of the Far West*, 9: 59.

had fled in terror. Twelve-year-old Jean-Baptiste may well have joined them, or—education having given him a degree of sophistication about science and technology—he could have watched watch in awe instead of fear.

Did Jean-Baptiste experience prejudice in St. Louis during this time of hostility towards Indians, or was he spared this humiliation since he was Clark's protégé and had taken on the ways of a white man? In either case, as he approached manhood, this young man who was the product of three different cultures, and perhaps not yet fully at home in any one of them, may well have longed to go West with his father to escape the rapidly changing city.

Duke Paul Wilhelm of Württemberg (1797-1860),
chalk drawing. (*Deutschordensmuseum, Bad Mergentheim=Museum
of the Teutonic Order, Bad Mergentheim*), *Foto: Deutschordensmuseum.*

Chapter Four

Duke Paul
of Württemberg

*An unquenchable thirst for knowledge drove him out into
the world.   —Friedrich Bauser*[1]

Jean-Baptiste's school days were drawing to an end. He was now a man of letters fit for any number of well-paying desk jobs in St. Louis. But the call of the north wind that had taken his parents back into the wilderness was also calling him. Perhaps as early as 1821, but certainly by the time he was eighteen in 1823, he escaped city life and set off to work for his godfather's family, the Chouteaus, and their Missouri Fur Company. The perfect opportunity to expand his world soon presented itself in the form of an unlikely kindred spirit, Friedrich Paul Wilhelm, duke of Württemberg, the second son of the brother of King Friedrich I of Württemberg, who had assumed the throne in 1806.[2] His family's royal connections were spread throughout Europe, and he was a nephew of Paul I, czar of Russia, as well as a cousin to czars

---
[1]John A. Hussey, ed. (*Early Sacramento: Glimpses*, 10), quotes Friedrich Bauser, the Stuttgart archivist who rediscovered Duke Paul's manuscripts about 1928, from Friedrich Bauser, "Biographical Facts Regarding Duke Paul of Wuerttemberg," 467; bear in mind, though, that Hans von Sachsen-Altenburg and Robert L. Dyer (*Duke Paul of Wuerttemberg on the Missouri Frontier*) caution that neither Bauser's nor Butscher's translations can be fully trusted.
[2]Although Duke Paul is often referred to in American publications as "Prince Paul," Albert Furtwangler ("Sacagawea's Son as a Symbol," n.28) clarifies that Paul's title was *Herzog* (Duke) rather than *Fürst* or *Prinz*.

Nicolas I and Alexander I. He was also distantly related to William II, king of England.

He is said to have explained his reason for going to St. Louis as:

> In the atmosphere of a palace I would feel like a wild thing that is imprisoned in a gilded cage. The ermine, the scepters, and the crown would be to me the emblems of a galley slave, and my heart would never cease to hunger for the vast silent places and the simple life among free unaffected children of nature.[3]

Duke Paul possessed an excellent education, a great love for natural science and ethnology, and a devotion to the hunt—interests that were in harmony with those of Jean-Baptiste, even though their beginnings could not have been more different. Such men, regardless of the circumstances of their birth, were drawn by their shared nature to the freedom and challenge of the unspoiled wild lands of the American West.

Like Jean-Baptiste's mentor, William Clark, Duke Paul was a man of the Enlightenment. New ideas of equality, wafting into musty, old German castles from France and America, had captivated him as a youth, putting him at odds with his uncle, King Frederick I, who eschewed all democratic notions. And there was also that "unquenchable thirst for knowledge [that] drove him out into the world."[4] He resigned his military commission and devoted himself to the study of zoology and botany under the finest German teach-

---

[3] Hussey, ed., *Early Sacramento: Glimpses*, 10 n.10; Ann W. Hafen, "Jean-Baptiste Charbonneau, 82 n.9, from Louis Butscher, *New Mexico Historical Review* 17 (1942): 190. Albert Furtwangler ("Sacagawea's Son as a Symbol," n.34) states that this "remark about being trapped in a palace is part of a patently fictitious anecdote." See Hussey, ed. (*Early Sacramento: Glimpses*, 22–25), as to the problems with Butscher's translations and inventions.

[4] Hussey, ed., *Early Sacramento: Glimpses*, 10; and see note 1, above. There were other motivations for his travels as well. Hussey speculates that by the time of his return to America in 1829, the duke was escaping an unhappy home situation. Von Sachsen-Altenburg and Dyer (*Duke Paul of Wuerttemberg on the Missouri Frontier*, 27) agree, calling his marriage of 1827 "disastrous." They believe the 1850 trip was to escape creditors. Others suggest, although there is no evidence for it, that he may have had an eye open for a possible German settlement in the West (Hussey, ed., *Early Sacramento: Glimpses*, 10 n.10).

ers. In 1822, instead of taking his rightful position in the newly formed House of Lords, he set sail on October 17 for North America in search of knowledge and adventure.[5] This would be the first of his three trips to the New World.

Duke Paul was just twenty-five in the spring of 1823 when he first arrived in St. Louis. Having studied the land and life ways of Cuba and New Orleans for the previous few months and now eager to explore the Mississippi and beyond, he had applied to the superintendent of Indian Affairs, William Clark, for a permit to visit the lands along the Missouri and the Columbia. When Clark asked his purpose, Duke Paul replied that his journey had "for its sole object my own instruction and ... the improvement of botany and natural history."[6] William Clark immediately identified with these Enlightenment goals. A military man himself, Clark must have been impressed, as well, with the discipline of this young man, already a colonel in the king's mounted guard. On May 6, 1823, while he was still in St. Louis, Duke Paul also accepted an invitation to the Chouteau estate. Thus, in mid-May, permit in hand, he set out from St. Charles, Missouri, by keelboat for a Chouteau trading post on the Kaw River, run by Cyrus Curtis and Andrew Woods, a journey of about five hundred miles up the Missouri.

Meetings with *Les Charbonneaux, Père et Fils*

Duke Paul's first meeting with Jean-Baptiste, a month later on June 21, was probably not a coincidence. Did Clark see this expedition as a way for his ward to continue his education? Most likely it was Clark himself and/or the Chouteaus who directed the prince to Clark's ward, who was

---
[5]Von Sachsen-Altenburg and Dyer, *Duke Paul of Wuerttemberg on the Missouri*, 39.
[6]Hussey, ed., *Early Sacramento: Glimpses*, 10; from "First Journal to North America in the years 1822–1824," translated by William G. Bek, in *South Dakota Historical Collections* 1938: 268.

then trading near the mouth of the Kaw River in present-day Kansas City, Kansas. Duke Paul describes their meeting:

> The settlements of the fur-traders, two spacious dwelling houses, are found a short half-mile farther on the right bank of the Missouri, and I rode thither in order to visit their respective owners.... The entire population of the settlement consisted of but a few persons, Creoles and half-breeds, whose occupation is the trading with Kansas Indians, confined mostly to the chase and the cultivation of the soil.
> Here I found a youth of sixteen, whose mother was of the tribe of Sho-sho-ne, or Snake Indians, and who had accompanied the Messrs. Lewis and Clark to the Pacific ocean in the years 1804 to 1806 a interpretress. This Indian woman was married to the French interpreter of the expedition, Toussaint Charbonneau by name. Charbonneau rendered me service also, some time later in the same capacity, and Baptiste, his son (the youth of sixteen) of whom I made mention above, joined me on my return and followed me to Europe, and has remained with me ever since.[7]

And so, these two young men, both possessed of a love of knowledge and natural places, began a friendship that would last many years.

That summer, Toussaint Charbonneau had been working at Fort Kiowa as a Gros Ventre interpreter. When the news arrived at the fort that a distinguished visitor was approaching, Toussaint was sent out by the clerk to invite the duke for a visit. Soon afterwards, Toussaint was hired by Duke Paul as a guide. Again, it is unlikely that this encounter was a coincidence. William Clark, lifelong friend of Toussaint, had probably recommended him.

Duke Paul's plan to reach the Columbia proved too ambitious. Because of Arikara hostilities in the West, he had to settle for Fort Kiowa as his furthest point of exploration. As summer was turning to fall, Toussaint and the duke headed

---

[7] Actually Jean-Baptiste was eighteen at the time, not sixteen. From H. P. Howard, *Sacagawea*, 170–71, quoted from William G. Bek, trans., "First Journal to America in the years 1822–1824," in *South Dakota Historical Collections* 1938.

east, picking up Jean-Baptiste at his Kaw River post on October 9. By then, a new plan had been hatched. Jean-Baptiste was to be Duke Paul's protégé. They would return to Germany together, where the young American could expand his knowledge of the world by studying abroad and traveling with the duke. In exchange, the duke would learn more about the American experience from Jean-Baptiste.[8]

Most likely, both of his fathers, Toussaint Charbonneau and William Clark, had given their approval to the plan. Clark must have been reminded of his own relationship with his adored eldest brother, the Revolutionary War hero George Rogers Clark, eighteen years his senior. Whereas George had grown up in Virginia and received a classical education, the Clark family had moved to the wilds of Kentucky by the time William was fourteen. This youngest brother, the last of the six Clark boys, had longed for a better education, but he had had to settle for educating himself as best he could. George had been particularly devoted to the study of natural history and science, and this had made a great impression on William. Although Meriwether Lewis is generally remembered as the more scholarly and William Clark as the more physical, in reality, Clark was very interested in natural science, collecting much of the expedition data. Indeed, he was eager to continue his research upon his return and, in 1807, had jumped at Jefferson's suggestion that he excavate fossils at Big Bones Lick, Kentucky.[9] Like Clark's brother George, Duke Paul's superior education, devotion to natural science, and achievements as a military man inspired Clark's admiration. What better role model for his gifted ward? Foremost in the minds of both Toussaint and Clark, however, may have been the potential for perfecting the lin-

---
[8]See Albert Furtwangler, "Sacagawea's Son: New Evidence from Germany."
[9]Jerome O. Steffen, *William Clark: Jeffersonian Man on the Frontier*, 14–15.

guistic studies Jean-Baptiste had begun during his school years. If he could fine-tune his ear to several European languages, future career opportunities would be enhanced.

Duke Paul was not concerned with Jean-Baptiste's lowly birth; nor was his motivation in inviting Jean-Baptiste to accompany him to Germany to employ him as a servant or show him off as an American savage. Heinrich Möllhausen, a noted German artist and novelist who accompanied the duke later in his life,[10] gives us this insight into the Paul he knew:

> The duke is a man of intellectuality far beyond ordinary comprehension. But his weak point is impulsiveness. His courage is so boundless that it often approaches downright madness itself. In spite of his early bringing up at one of the most exclusive royal courts in Christendom he is utterly democratic and considerate in all his dealings with others.[11]

Duke Paul, then, admired the Jeffersonian ideals of racial harmony and a classless society. He often mentioned his admiration for the American Founding Fathers in his journals, and he was said to be content to be his own valet.[12] Like Clark, he believed in the brotherhood of mankind, and, like Jean-Baptiste's French professors, Paul too had probably been influenced by Rousseau's romantic ideal of the "noble savage." And who could be a more romantic symbol of that ideal than Sacagawea's son, the Indian infant who had accompanied the Corps of Discovery? Duke Paul sought in Jean-Baptiste the "unaffected child of nature," so much more appealing to him than the jaded youths of aristocratic court life. Also, he would be able to learn about Native

---

[10] Hebard (*Sacajawea*, 147) names Möllhausen as the artist who painted a portrait of Paul and Jean-Baptiste among the Kansas Indians. Furtwangler ("Sacagawea's Son: New Evidence from Germany," 518–20), however, makes a persuasive case for Duke Paul himself as the artist. See page 30 for this illustration.

[11] A. W. Hafen, "Jean-Baptiste Charbonneau," 81–82 n.8, from *New Mexico Historical Review* 17 (1942): 190.   [12] Hussey, ed., *Early Sacramento: Glimpses*, 9.

American ethnology and linguistics from this lad who had lived among the Mandan, Hidatsa, and Kansas Indians. As German researcher Monika Frida suggests, the duke probably expected to gain as much from these relationships as he bestowed upon his protégés.[13] We might also deduce that Jean-Baptiste had lost none of the charm and charisma that had drawn William Clark to him as a baby. Duke Paul could see the promise in the lad.

Jean-Baptiste was not his only protégé, however. Over the years, Duke Paul brought back several foreign boys from his various travels, including a mixed blood Mexican, two Africans, and a "small Indian" named Antonio. Duke Paul's treatment of the Mexican, Johann (Juan) Alvarado, may shed light on how Jean-Baptiste fared. Juan arrived in Germany just two years after Jean-Baptiste had returned to America. In the duke's records, it is clear that he managed Juan's agenda; one could say that Juan "served at the pleasure of the court." Juan did, however, acquire ownership of some jewels, silks, and satins. His schoolbooks show he was tutored in geography, history, arithmetic, French, and Spanish. Letters reveal he had learned some German, as well as the craft of bookbinding, and that he supervised a few underlings and helped with such activities as setting off festive fireworks. He was paid enough in wages to accumulate some savings. When he died after ten years in Germany, the duke paid his debts and gave him a proper burial. The lad was not labeled by race and was not put on display. When Juan had an affair with an unmarried woman and fathered a

---

[13]Furtwangler, "Sacagawea's Son New Evidence from Germany," 521–22, n.18. The data in this paragraph are paraphrased from Furtwangler's account of the research in Germany of Monika Firla. Also see Monica Firla, "Die anonyme Gouache 'Herzog Paul von Württemberg bei den Indianern' und die neuentdeckte Lithographie 'Lager der Kanzas am blauen Fluss, den 3ten Juli 1823. Häuptlinge Wakan-zie und Sa-ba-No-sche' nach einer Zeichnung des Herzogs," *Württembergisch Franken: Jahrbuch des Historischen Vereins für Württembergish Franken* 84 (2000): 259–87.

child, he feared this indiscretion would displease his mentor, but the question of "mixed blood" was not perceived as the problem. In any case, since taking a mistress was accepted behavior, the duke was not shocked by Juan's transgression. Indeed, Duke Paul himself was said to have had at least one mistress and one illegitimate child over the years.[14]

An American in Europe, 1824–1829

On November 3, 1823, after spending ten days in St. Louis saying their good-byes, the two young men, nephews of a king of the Old World and an Indian chief of the New, set off for New Orleans. The trip got off to a poor start, however, when their steamboat, *Cincinnati*, grounded on a sandbar and promptly sank in the Mississippi. Fortunately, all aboard were able to scramble ashore in time. The travelers finally arrived in New Orleans six weeks after their initial departure. Jean-Baptiste must have been entranced by the sights of this city, boasting well over 27,000 inhabitants, by far the largest he had ever seen. And Duke Paul must have enjoyed showing it off to his protégé, as its food, lifestyle, and hospitable citizenry had already made New Orleans his favorite city in America.[15] These two eager young travellers did not have much time to enjoy its many charms, however. Their ship, the *Smyra*, was scheduled to set sail for Le Havre, France, on December 23, just two days later. On that Sunday morning, the young travelers boarded the handsome, three-masted, coppered brig for the beginning of their five-and-a-half-year adventure abroad. Celebrating Christmas by waiting for fair winds in the mosquito- and alligator-infested Mississippi, however, may have dampened their spirits some, but not for long. At last they were off!

---

[14]Von Sachsen-Altenburg and Dyer, *Duke Paul of Wuerttemberg on the Missouri Frontier*, 87.
[15]See A. W. Hafen, "Jean-Baptiste Charbonneau," 80.

A sea crossing in winter was Jean-Baptiste's first challenge. This, his first sighting of the Atlantic had occurred almost exactly eighteen years after his first sighting of the Pacific, when his mother was nearly the same age he was now.[16] The excitement of travel probably helped ease his discomfort in the tossing seas until, on February 14, 1824, just three days after his nineteenth birthday, the two friends finally set foot on the French soil Jean-Baptiste's ancestors had left 165 years before.

They must have been the talk of the town. This was not the return of some anonymous young traveler. Duke Paul was one of the wealthiest men in Europe and a celebrity, as well, with "his doings reasonably well known to readers of the world press."[17] And here he was, back from more than a year abroad, with an exotic American in his entourage.

Unfortunately, the details of those five and a half years in Europe are not accessible,[18] but we do know that Jean-Baptiste, born in a rough fort on the Missouri, spent most of the following few years in the duke's enormous eleventh-century castle in the vast woodlands about thirty miles from Stuttgart.[19] Here, as he traveled the old Roman roads of ancient Württemberg, he found a context for his schoolroom studies of Classical through post-Napoleonic Europe. He also acquired a "classic education" and improved upon his language training from St. Louis Academy, mastering German, Spanish, English, and French. Duke Paul was an ideal language tutor for him, having excelled in linguistics as a student in Stuttgart. Jean-Baptiste could practice his

---

[16]After pleading with Clark to let her accompany the party going to the ocean, she finally saw it on January 7, 1806. [17]Hussey, ed., *Early Sacramento: Glimpses*, 7.

[18]Journals were kept but most await trustworthy translation. Although some may have been destroyed in WWII bombings, Von Sachsen-Altenburg and Dyer (*Duke Paul of Wuerttemberg on the Missouri Frontier*, 26) report that "papers thought to have been lost have recently been found."

[19]A. W. Hafen, "Jean-Baptiste Charbonneau," 81; Von Sachsen-Altenburg and Dyer, *Duke Paul of Wuerttemberg on the Missouri Frontier*, 26, 36.

improving skills as they traveled together, not only in Germany, but also in France, England, and maybe as far as Africa.[20] Just drinking in the culture of Beethoven's times would have been an extraordinary education in itself. In the practical arts, Jean-Baptiste could also benefit from Duke Paul's expertise with firearms, horses, and hunting. The two hunted together in the Black Forest where Jean-Baptiste, called "hunter extraordinary" by his new mentor, impressed the duke with his abilities.[21]

This carefree bachelor existence was about to take a dramatic turn in 1827 when Duke Paul, now thirty, married Princess Sophie Dorothea Caroline of Thurn and Taxis. The 400-plate affair in the grand hall of the castle must have made an impression on young Jean-Baptiste. Soon the entire household, including the American guest, was removed to nearby Mergentheim, which remained Paul's home for the next thirty years. Unfortunately, the duke and his princess did not live happily ever after. By the following year, when Duke Paul's son Duke Maximilian was born, Sophie had left the duke and was living in a castle belonging to her own family. Separated from his wife and infant son, Duke Paul's thoughts returned to happier days in the wilderness of the upper Missouri.

Jean-Baptiste had also suffered losses of love. Records recently discovered by Firla in Germany reveal that, like Juan Alvarado, who followed him at court, Jean-Baptiste also had a child with an unmarried woman. Anton Fries was the child of "Johann Baptist Charbonnau of St Louis 'called the American' in the service of Duke Paul of this place and

---

[20] Although it is widely quoted that Jean-Baptiste accompanied Duke Paul to Africa, the duke is not known to have traveled there until 1839, long after his association with Jean-Baptiste. However, the travels of the two men between 1824 and 1829 are so poorly documented that we cannot say with any certainty if they made it to Africa—to see the original Pompey's Pillar—or not.   [21] A. W. Hafen, "Jean-Baptiste Charbonneau," 82.

Aerial photo of the former castle of the Teutonic Order in Bad Mergentheim. Duke Paul and Jean-Baptiste lived on the top floor of the west wing; see Von Sachsen-Altenberg and Dyer, *Duke Paul of Wuerttemberg on the Missouri Frontier 1823, 1830 and 1851*, p. 36. Foto: Luftbild Bytomski, Würzburg.

Anastasia Katharina Fries, unmarried daughter of the late Georg Fries, a soldier here."[22] This is Jean-Baptiste's only documented liaison and only known child. No record of his reaction to the birth and death of his three-month-old son have ever been found. He may not have even been in Germany when his son died, since it was in that same month of May that Jean-Baptiste and Duke Paul began their return trip west. This final European trip together began with a visit to Paris, followed by Bordeaux, and ending in the Basque country of Spain.[23]

---

[22]Furtwangler, "Sacagawea's Son New Evidence from Germany." Originally from Monika Firla, "Johan Alvarado (1815–41), Ein mexikanischer Kammerdiener Herzog Paul Wilhelm von Württemberg in Mergentheim," *Württembergisch Franken: Jahrbuch des Historischen Vereins für Württembergish Franken* 83 (1999): 247–60, quotation 248 n.3, translated by Furtwangler. Anton Fries was born on February 20, 1829, and died on May 15, 1829.

[23]Von Sachsen-Altenburg and Dyer, *Duke Paul of Wuerttemberg on the Missouri Frontier*, 83.

Return to America

From there, they left their personal problems behind, sailing west again after nearly six years abroad. Their first stop was San Domingo in the West Indies, where they arrived on August 5, 1829. They proceeded on to several Caribbean islands and then to New Orleans, arriving in St. Louis on December 1. Jean-Baptiste had left St. Louis as a boy and now returned as a man of the world. Not wishing to tarry in the city, the travelers were granted the permission they sought by Clark and soon headed back up the river once more. On December 23, 1829, the exact anniversary of their departure for Europe six years before, the small expedition of Duke Paul (traveling as Baron von Hohenberg), two servants, a clerk named Zierlein, and "Mr. John Baptist"[24] set off for Council Bluffs and Fort Atkinson to hunt and trade. The following February, they pressed on for the Mandan villages and Fort Clark. On May 19, 1830, they were at Fort Union and still together. Not long afterwards, however, Jean-Baptiste struck off on his own to join the fur trade. The journal of a fellow traveler, Warren A. Ferris, places him with the Rubidoux Fur Brigade that spring. Meanwhile, Duke Paul remained on the Missouri, hunting and trading between Council Bluffs and Fort Union for over a year, not returning to New Orleans until November 1831.

Here the record of the association of Duke Paul and Jean-Baptiste Charbonneau comes to a sudden end. We may never know the reason—no journals by the duke for that journey have been found. Jean-Baptiste may have been ready to begin his life as a self-supporting man, free of his mentors. We do know that Duke Paul spent the following two years in the United States and the Caribbean before returning to Württemberg, but would return many years later to the United States.

---

[24]Ibid., 84.

Chapter Five

MOUNTAIN MAN

... and I defy the annals of chivalry to furnish the record of a life more wild and perilous than that of a Rocky Mountain trapper.   —Francis Parkman, 1846[1]

Jean-Baptiste's contemporaries provide some clues as to his personality and character. Rufus B. Sage, a New Englander traveling in the West from 1841 to 1844, gave this revealing portrait in his journal entry of August 30, 1842:

> The camp was under the direction of a half-breed, named Chabonard, who proved to be a gentleman of superior information. He had acquired a classic education and could converse quite fluently in German, Spanish, French and English, as well as several Indian languages. His mind, also, was well stored with choice reading, and enriched by extensive travel and observation. Having visited most of the important places, both in England, France, and Germany, he knew how to turn his experience to good advantage.
> There was a quaint humor and shrewdness in his conversation, so garbed with intelligence and perspicuity, that he at once insinuated himself into the good graces of listeners, and commanded their admiration and respect.... About noon we bade farewell to our new friends, by whom we had been kindly entertained."[2]

Jean-Baptiste did, however, have a rough-hewn side, living by the rules of a frontier society formulated by and for men of action. William Clark Kennerly, nephew of Captain

---
[1] Parkman, *The Oregon Trail*, 118.
[2] Rufus B. Sage, *Rocky Mountain Life*, 206.

William Clark, wrote of a dramatic western scene he witnessed in 1843:

> Later there was a fight between Walker and Smith, and the whole cavalcade stopped to witness it, while Charbonneau ran excitedly about, keeping a ring around the combatants with his heavy whip and shouting for no one to interfere. It was not a very even fight; Smith was much the larger man, but, after a few rounds when he jumped on Walker's back in an effort to bear him to the ground, Walker drew his pistol and, firing over his shoulder, wounded Smith in the thigh, the wonder being that he did not kill him.[3]

Other journals of the time provide an idea of his physical appearance and prowess. The following three conjure an image of a striking man who was confident, fit, and dependable. Williams Boggs, son of Gov. L. W. Boggs of Missouri, wrote in 1844:

> This Baptiste Charbenau, or half-breed son of the elder Charbenau that was employed by the Lewis and Clark expedition to the Pacific Ocean, had been educated to some extent; he wore his hair long so that it hung down to his shoulders. It is said that Charbenau was the best man on foot on the plains or in the Rocky Mountains.[4]

In 1846, Mormon Battalion leader Col. Phillip St. George Cooke described him as "humanity in confusion . . . near gentleman, near animal but above all capable, loyal and a most valued asset."[5] George F. Ruxton, an English traveler and writer, described the best of the Mountain Men in 1848 and said of Jean-Baptiste, "Charbonar, a half-breed, was not lost in the crowd."[6]

---

[3] Kennerly and Russell, *Persimmon Hill*, 158.
[4] *William M. Boggs Journal, 1844–1845*, quoted in Harold P. Howard, *Sacajawea*, 173.
[5] Joseph B. Frazier, "Charbonneau saw world, worked in many trades," quoting Cooke's journal.
[6] The quote by George F. Ruxton (Hebard, *Sacajawea*, 144) is usually reproduced to include a longer description of Jean-Baptiste as "last in height but first in every quality which constitutes excellence in a mountaineer . . . who was 'taller' for his inches than Kit Carson." The shorter quote I reproduce in the present text is the only part of Ruxton's quote that actually refers to Jean-Baptiste. A careful reading of the rest of Ruxton's quote (*Life*

Such assessments of Jean-Baptiste were repeated in many of the journals of the time as he worked as interpreter-hunter-trader-guide to high praise for the next fifteen years. Where his father was all rough edges, he was polished. Education had made the difference.[7] He did not strive to fit in. He had the confidence to be one of a kind, a gentleman *métis* mountaineer. Many see him as an anomaly. The art to Jean-Baptiste's life was the choice he made to live the free life he loved while still letting his education inform his thoughts and behaviors. In other words, he melded the three cultures of his upbringing to create a unique man—French-Indian-Enlightened. Living among the upper classes in Europe, he had seen what money could provide, but this had not turned his head. What he wanted out of life was just what he got, and is this not the definition of a successful and fulfilling life? His old friend and fellow Mountain Man, Jim Beckwourth, summed it up eloquently: "... the Indian was ineffaceable in him. The Indian lodge and his native fastnesses possessed greater charms than the luxuries of civilized life."[8]

Did his superior education set him apart and make him an object of derision among his mostly illiterate fellow Mountain Men? In truth, as the above quote of Rufus Sage indicates, there was a lot of respect on the trail for educated men. In the journals of others, Jean-Baptiste was never derided for his erudition. In fact, during their long periods of inactivity, the men often sought to educate one another in what they called the "Rocky Mountain College." Joe Meek,

---

in the Far West, 183) reveals that the description following "Chabonard a half-breed, was not lost in the crowd," refers to Kit Carson and not to Jean-Baptiste. This becomes clear if it is noted that the quote ends in a question mark. Following "Chabonard a half-breed, was not lost in the crowd," Ruxton asks, "who was not 'taller' for his inches than Kit Carson, paragon of mountaineers?" He is asking this about Kit Carson; he is not saying that Jean-Baptiste was taller for his inches than Kit Carson.

[7]Rogers (*Lewis and Clark in Missouri*, 111) points out that Toussaint signed Jean-Baptiste's baptismal record with an 'X.'

[8]Thomas D. Bonner, *The Life and Adventures of James P. Beckwourth*, 528.

for example, was known for his intellectual curiosity, and although illiterate, Jim Bridger would pass on his wealth of wilderness lore orally, while men of letters, like Jean-Baptiste, would read aloud and tell stories of life in far-off places. These outposts so far from civilization cherished their Bibles and volumes of Shakespeare, Byron, Scott, and others, and these works were discussed at length. Many of the men, like Joe Meek, were proud to recite long passages from memory and to name their children for the characters.[9]

Trapper Attire

An image of the adult Jean-Baptiste can be formed with knowledge of his trapper attire. Ruxton described the trapper's shirt as made of dressed buckskin ornamented with long fringes, along with pantaloons of the same material but decorated with porcupine quills and long fringes down the outside of the leg, plus a flexible felt hat for the head and leather moccasins for the feet.[10] Cleland added, "the deerskin shirt, when soaked, wrung out, and dried, became a veritable buckskin coat of mail that only the hardest driven Indian arrow would penetrate."[11] Sage described the leather belt holding the trapper's butcher knife and pistols, plus other necessities, including a bullet pouch and powder horn, a "gun-stick made of hard wood and a good rifle carrying from thirty-five balls to the pound."[12]

Although it is likely that Jean-Baptiste dressed like this at least part of the time, there are only two references to his clothing in the various journals of fellow travelers. The first is Joe Meek's mention of him in 1831 as looking like an Indian "with his shoulder-length black hair, worn buckskin and

---

[9]Tobie, "Joseph L. Meek," 358.
[10]Ruxton, G. F., *Life in the Far West*.
[11]R. G. Cleland, *This Restless Breed of Men*, 21.
[12]Sage, *Rocky Mountain Life*, 38.

beaded moccasins."[13] The second is fifteen years later, in the mountains along the Santa Fe Trail, when Cooke mentioned him wearing a red shirt.[14] In 1838, Toussaint was also described as wearing a red shirt.[15] Donning a bright color among so many hunters and otherwise armed men was a bit of wisdom that may have contributed to the long lives of both father and son.

Home on the Range

Jean-Baptiste was not a man to settle down before he was too old for the trail. Perhaps he was satisfied with the roving life on the prairies and in the mountains because of its compelling compensations. As Rufus Sage put it, "There is a charm in the loneliness—an enchantment in the solitude—a witching variety in the sameness, that must ever impress the traveler, when, for the first time, he enters within the confines of the great western prairies."[16] Some were awed but felt compelled to move on and find a place to settle; while others, like Jean-Baptiste and his father, were seduced by the charm and the freedom of an unfettered life on the plains and in the mountains, and they found that they could never leave it. French-Canadians seemed more susceptible than most, as Francis Parkman found on his adventure to the Rockies in 1846:

> Mingled among the crowd of Indians was a number of Canadians, . . . —men whose home is the wilderness, and who love the camp-fire better than the domestic hearth. They are contented and happy in the midst of hardship, privation, and danger. Their

---

[13] Norman McLeod, "Heritage: Jean-Baptiste Charbonneau, Cultured Mountain Man," 21.
[14] Cooke, Phillip St. George, "Journal of the March of the Mormon Battalion," entry for November 25, 1846, 131, 134.
[15] L. R. Hafen, ed., *The Mountain Men and the Fur Trade of the Far West*, 9: 61. In 1838, Charles Larpenteur was relieved that the "Indian" approaching in a red shirt was really their interpreter, Toussaint Charbonneau.
[16] Sage, *Rocky Mountain Life*, 33.

cheerfulness and gayety is irrepressible, and no people on earth understand better how "to daff the world aside and bid it pass".[17]

We cannot know for sure, but perhaps Jean-Baptiste was the "educated Indian" with whom T. J. Farnham conversed at Fort El Pueblo near Bent's Fort in 1839. In any case, this alleged exchange suggests a possible rationale for Jean-Baptiste's life choices:

> "Why did you leave civilized life for a precarious livelihood in the wilderness?," asked Farnham.
>
> For reasons found in the nature of my race, [replied the trapper]. The Indian's eye cannot be satisfied with the *description* of things, how beautiful soever may be the style, or the harmonies of verse in which it is conveyed. For neither the periods of burning eloquence, nor the mighty and beautiful creations of the imagination, can unbosom the treasures and realities as they live in their own native magnificence on the eternal mountains, and in the secret untrodden vale. . . .
>
> I must range the hills, I must always be able to out-travel my horses, I must always be able to strip my own wardrobe from the backs of the deer and buffalo, and to feed upon their rich loins; I must always be able to punish my enemy with my own hand, or I am no longer an Indian.[18]

Jean-Baptiste saw nothing in the settlements that could match the freedom and beauty of the wild, open spaces. John C. Frémont described the valley of the Platte, where he found Jean-Baptiste in the summer of 1842, as a garden of fields of varied flowers and wild sage, filling the air with fragrance—"everywhere the rose is met with," scattered over the prairies in small bouquets.[19] The amorpha were in full bloom with large, luxuriant purple clusters of flowers, and wild sun-

---

[17]Parkman, *The Oregon Trail*, 249.

[18]T. J. Farnham in Thwaites, Reuben Gold, ed., "Farnham, Farnham's Travels," 28: 176, 179. This ornate language suggests some creative embellishment on Farnham's part, and some find it far-fetched to assume that he was referring to Jean-Baptiste. But how many "educated Indians" were there in the West (and specifically, at Bent's Fort) in 1839? Jean-Baptiste may have been unique at this time and place, increasing the likelihood that he was indeed Farnham's "educated Indian."

[19]John C. Frémont, *Report of the Exploring Expedition to the Rocky Mountains*, 14.

flowers were everywhere. Forming the backdrop to this glorious display were the splendid Black Hills. Parkman added, "the wild beasts and wild men that frequent the valley of the Platte make it a scene of interest and excitement to the traveler. Of those who have journeyed there, scarcely one, perhaps, fails to look back with fond regret to his horse and his rifle."[20] None of the trappings of civilization were present—only an occasional fort or Indian village. In this context, Jean-Baptiste's choice of this lifestyle was consistent with his upbringing and background.

His was a worldview consistent with the cultural values of his Indian and French-Canadian heritage. Less focused on acquisition than his Anglo counterpart, the French-Canadian Mountain Man did not require or seek the comforts. He could work hard for long hours in any weather, month after month, with minimal food and shelter and with an attitude generally less critical of and more loyal to authority. His disposition was more compatible with the Indians with whom he worked than with the Anglos.[21] Of course, there were the bourgeois French merchants who were ambitious for financial gains, but many of the lads of humbler origins, as well as those with Indian mothers, were content to accept life on the trail as its own reward.

Life of a Mountain Man

The prototype of the American Mountain Man was the intrepid Canadian *voyageur* and the explorers who, since the early seventeenth century, had blazed new trails westward.[22] These trails eventually covered much of present-day Canada as well as thirty-one American states. For

---

[20]Parkman, *The Oregon Trail*, 54.   [21]Faherty, *Dream by the River*, 59.
[22]Grace Nute (*The Voyageur*, 3) explains that the term *voyageur* initially included all explorers, fur-traders, and travelers, but it was later restricted to canoe- and boatmen for the fur trade. If a *voyageur* served at all as a fur trader, it was in a subordinate role to clerks and proprietors.

over two hundred years, the north wind had lured North American farm boys into the wilderness to trap and trade for furs, particularly for those of the beaver, which were in great demand in America and Europe during the late eighteenth and early nineteenth centuries. Until replaced by silk in the mid-1830s, the fine felt of the beaver pelt had been deemed a necessity by gentlemen's hatters. It seems incredible now that a top hat could topple empires, but that is exactly what happened—the economies of Canada and the United States rose and fell in response to this fad. Furs, in general, were big business. Beyond the 25,000 beaver pelts taken each year, there were also between 40,000 and 50,000 buffalo hides, 100,000 muskrats, between 20,000 and 30,000 deer, and thousands of otter, marten, lynx, fox, and mink.[23] The competition for these furs revolutionized the cultures of various whites and Indians from coast to coast until late in the nineteenth century.

Jean-Baptiste was immersed in this phenomenon from his birth and it remained the focal point of his life well into middle age. His father's presence on the Missouri River at the time of the boy's birth was solely because of the fur trade. In addition, a major purpose of the Corps of Discovery, in which Jean-Baptiste was the youngest participant, was to open western trade routes to American fur interests. His education in languages was meant to prepare him for fur trade work as an interpreter and guide, and all of his work in his prime, between the ages of twenty-four and thirty-nine, was in the fur trade business and associated activities for western exploration and expansion. When beaver and bison numbers declined and the fur trade was ending, men like Jean-Baptiste had to move on.

---

[23]Schierle, ed., *Travels in the Interior of North America*, 27, 166. The average price for a buffalo hide was four dollars.

A Mountain Man needed many skills and it took him many years to acquire them all—if he lived that long. This was a dangerous life that tolerated few errors. Even the best of men, like George Drouillard, who had been third in command of the expedition behind Lewis and Clark, often died violently. On fur-trading business for Manuel Lisa in 1810, Drouillard lost his life to the Blackfeet, who were still enraged by the shooting of two of their men by Meriwether Lewis. Many other Mountain Men drowned while transporting furs or were done in by thieves, wild animals, hostile raiders, or the elements. A sixth sense was required to distinguish friend from foe. For example, just as Jean-Baptiste was beginning his new life in 1830, three other traders were killed by Arikaras, who had just smoked with them and had shown every sign of peaceful intent.[24] Besides good luck and judgment, a Mountain Man had to have strength and endurance and be adept at finding his way, both on land and on water, through chartless wilderness. It was essential that he be able to communicate with Indians of many language families, using signs, words, and/or smoke signals. And he needed to maintain friendly relations with them and his fellow mountaineers. This multi-cultural world was not for the bigoted: "The Mountain Men were ... more open-minded and sensitive to other cultural viewpoints than any other social group entering the West during the nineteenth century."[25]

He also had to keep his horse or mule fed and healthy, hunt, trap, butcher, process skins, and maintain and create all manner of tools and essentials. Plus, he had to be able to read the weather and the landscape and either prevent or survive enemy and animal attacks, days without food and

---

[24] J. F. A. Sanford to William Clark, October 20, 1830 (William Clark Papers, Kansas State Historical Society).
[25] Harvey L. Carter, "Introduction," xviii, quoting William R. Swagerty, "Marriage and Settlement Patterns of Rocky Mountain Trappers and Traders," 159–80.

water, extremes in cold and heat, isolation and loneliness, and the orneriness of his mules and fellow mountaineers. If he had no wife to assist him and look after him, he had to be able to procure all his own food, cook it in all weather, transport all of his gear, entertain himself, and nurse his wounds and illnesses without help. He needed the discipline and good humor not to drown himself in a bottle to escape his loneliness and pain. And he had to be able to sleep wet and cold and then get up at dawn and work hard until dusk in rain and snow and dust and all manner of misery—day after day and month after month. But mainly he had to have a gift for finding the joy and humor in it all so that he could keep the passion alive to sign on again for another year. It is no wonder Harvey Carter concluded of the Mountain Men, "They had the right stuff."[26]

The Upper Missouri Fur Trade by 1830

Jean-Baptiste had been introduced to the fur trading life while still a teenager, but it was not until his return from Europe that he took up his career in earnest. He was just a notch above a greenhorn with a lot to learn when he joined the American Fur Company's 1830 spring expedition.

The fur business was then thriving—largely because of the efforts of Jean-Baptiste's guardian, William Clark. Although St. Louis had been a fur trading hub since 1794, it was not until Lewis and Clark had opened the way by finding routes and establishing good relations with the Indians that the St. Louis fur trade really got underway. Beyond obvious mercantile considerations, the American fur enterprise was seen by Jefferson and Clark as the glue essential for binding the West to the United States, rather than to Eng-

---

[26]Harvey L. Carter, "Introduction," xviii.

land, for only by monopolizing the fur trade could America hope to stop the growing influence of England in the West. Whereas George Rogers Clark had secured the lands east of the Mississippi River for the United States, now it was the turn of his youngest brother to make sure that the lands to its west were similarly secured.

Recall that it was part of the Enlightenment philosophy that the public good be the focus of commercial, political, and scientific interests, and that these elements work together to assure America's success. That is why it was not considered a conflict of interest for Clark to become an organizing founder of the Missouri Fur Company and to personally invest heavily in it. In the Jeffersonian view, if investments made by public officials profited the public as well as themselves, then the ideal outcome had been achieved.[27]

That Clark had such investment opportunities on his mind (both for himself and for his associates) upon his return from the Corps of Discovery expedition is evident in his letter to Toussaint Charbonneau soon after he left him in 1806: ". . . if you wish to return to trade with the indians . . . I will assist you with merchandise for the purpose and become my self concerned with you in trade on a small scale that is to say not exceeding a perogue load at one time."[28]

But Clark knew that only large-scale efforts would bring the desired results. He encouraged both the formation of the St. Louis Fur Company by the Chouteaus in the winter of 1808–09 and the development of the Missouri Fur Company by Manuel Lisa from 1807 to 1811. Initially, these efforts met with success, and by 1811, over three hundred trappers were already working in the Columbia River region. Toussaint

---

[27]Steffen (*William Clark Jeffersonian Man on the Frontier*, 5–7) explains well how these values were interconnected in Jeffersonian philosophy.
[28]Thwaites, *Original Journals*, 7: 329.

Charbonneau had jumped on this bandwagon in 1811 and 1812, and that is why he and Sacagawea were at Manuel Lisa's fort when disaster struck; she died of a fever and he was caught up in the consequences of war. Years of halted fur traffic and economic hardship had come with the war, but recovery was finally underway in 1815, mainly through the efforts of Ninian Edwards, William Clark, and Jean-Baptiste's godfather, Auguste Chouteau. These men and others of like mind set to work to establish the fur trade dominance believed essential to prevent another rise to power by the British.

Four St. Louis companies were in competition in the 1820s: the Missouri Fur Company, the Rocky Mountain Fur Company, the Columbia Fur Company, and the American Fur Company. But it was the latter that soon became dominant. A big boost to the St. Louis companies came in 1821 when Mexico won its independence from Spain and lifted its trade embargo against the United States. This first "free trade agreement" between the two countries stimulated trade in all kinds of goods between America and Mexico by way of the Santa Fe Trail. Another boost to St. Louis trade in 1821 was the merger in British Canada of the Hudson's Bay Company with the North West Fur Company. This resulted in the southward migration of many experienced fur traders and the subsequent strengthening of the St. Louis companies at the expense of England's.

1830 & 1831: Jean-Baptiste Sets Out with the American Fur Company

By Jean-Baptiste's re-entry into the trade in 1830, competition was hot. Two companies had left St. Louis that spring: the American Fur Company's Robidoux Fur Brigade under the direction of Lucien Fontenelle, Andrew Drips, and Joseph Robidoux, and its rival, the company headed by William Sublette (soon to be called the Rocky Mountain Fur Company). Jean-Baptiste was with the former as they followed the muddy Platte, crossed it in their bull hide canoes, and forged on to the Black Hills.[29] As they followed the river systems into the Rockies, Jean-Baptiste got his first glimpse of the wild places that would become very familiar to him over the next few years, like Green River, site of most of the legendary rendezvous of the 1830s.

Both companies hoped to be the first to arrive at these rendezvous and meet up with the trappers who had been gathering furs all winter and spring. The company that could outfit the trappers for the new season, help them spend their earnings, and provide items of trade for the Indians and plenty of liquor would be the big winner for that year. Timing was everything, as the window of opportunity lasted only about two weeks. In their eagerness to be first at the Wind River rendezvous in the summer of 1830, Drips and Fontenelle arrived in June—too early to find the trappers. They had to cache their supplies and begin their own fall hunt. When Sublette arrived July 4, the spoils were his and he hosted the gathering.

Jean-Baptiste must have missed this first chance to attend a rendezvous, for he spent that summer and fall working in the area that would eventually become Idaho and Utah. By November, he was trapping various tributaries of the Snake River with Michel Robidoux, after which he and some others attempted to make their way to Cache Valley for the winter. This proved to be an important learning experience for the inexperienced Jean-Baptiste when an unwisely cho-

---

[29] Warren Angus Ferris, *Life in the Rocky Mountains*, 64. Ferris' accounts are questioned by some scholars; see, for example, Irving W. Anderson (papers, Special Collections, Lewis and Clark College, Portland, Oregon). Others, like A. W. Hafen ("Jean-Baptiste Charbonneau") and Harold P. Howard (*Sacajawea*) quote him freely.

sen route nearly led them to disaster. The men had tried going northwest from American Falls to Wood River, which meant crossing forty miles of desiccated lava beds and the aptly-named Craters of the Moon. The lack of water, exacerbated by a diet of dried meat, and the relentless heat, brought crippling thirst. But the worst was yet to come, as a huge fissure suddenly materialized before them, stopping them in their tracks. There was no solution but to backtrack across the barren landscape. In a desperate two-day search for water, Jean-Baptiste became separated from the others. At last, he found a river, the Maladi, but he mistook a camp there of John Work's Hudson's Bay Company Snake Brigade for an Indian camp and he avoided it. Unbeknownst to him, his fellow travelers had taken refuge there, where they were relaxing in comfort, while he trudged on in misery. In later years, he must have looked back and laughed at his early experiences in the Far West, but this first misadventure, recorded by one of the trappers who had sojourned with John Work, was not very funny at the time:

> We returned to Cache Valley by the way of Porteneuf, where we found Dripps and Fontenelle, together with our lost companion Charbineaux. He states that he lost our trail, but reached the river Maladi after dark, where he discovered a village of Indians. Fearing that they were unfriendly, he resolved to retrace his steps, and find the main company. In pursuance of this plan, he filled a bear skin with water, and set off on his lonely way. After eleven days' wandering, during which he suffered a good deal from hunger, he attained his object, and reached the company at Porteneuf.[30]

Fortunately, Jean-Baptiste had plenty of time to reflect and recover at winter camp. It was during that same severe winter of 1830–31 that legendary mountain man Joe Meek, then just twenty years of age, was wintering with Thomas

---

[30]Ferris, *Life in the Rocky Mountains*, 67; T. C. Elliot, "Journal of John Work," 368–70.

Fitzpatrick on the Powder River. He and a fellow trapper, named Legarde, were chosen to take a dispatch to St. Louis. They soon ran into trouble and Legarde was taken prisoner by the Pawnees. Meek then had to proceed alone, but he had the good fortune to cross paths with an eastbound express willing to take his message for him. Relieved of this duty, he was pleasantly surprised to encounter "a Frenchman, Cabenau" (believed to be Jean-Baptiste) at the mouth of the Platte. Meek nearly mistook him for an Indian "with his shoulder length black hair, worn buckskin and beaded moccasins."[31] Grateful for the company, the two young men returned to the Rockies together.

The rivalry between the St. Louis fur companies continued as the years went on. In the summer of 1831, it was the Rocky Mountain Fur Company that suffered. Its guide, the renowned Jedediah Smith, was killed by Comanches while trying to cross the Cimarron Desert, and his company was not able to get supplies to the rendezvous. The American Fur Company fared better when Etienne Provost brought their supplies west that summer. Jean-Baptiste may have been there to greet him, but his activities in 1831 after his encounter with Meek are not known.

Trapping by the Skin

In the summer of 1832, the mountaineers met at Pierre's Hole, considered by Jim Bridger to be "the finest valley in the mountains."[32] This basin is located in present-day Idaho, just across Teton Pass from Jackson Hole and near the headwaters of the Snake River. With a width spanning ten miles and a length about seventy, visibility seems limitless. Its

---

[31]Harold P. Howard, *Sacajawea*, 171; Frances Fuller Victor, *The River of the West*, 96; McLeod, "Heritage: Jean-Baptiste Charbonneau," 21.
[32]Vestal, *Jim Bridger Mountain Man*, 69.

beauty is enhanced by a lovely cottonwood- and willow-lined river, which ribbons through its smooth plains. The mountains that frame it are so high to the east and west that they are nearly impenetrable. With such protection, this was indeed an excellent choice for the safety of the various fur traders, Indians, and *métis* assembling from throughout the mountains with their fur-laden horses. Soon Indian lodges were rising along the river and campsites dotted the landscape. This rendezvous of 1832 was to be the largest party of Mountain Men and Indians ever assembled. By the time all had congregated, there would be about a thousand men, with perhaps triple that number of mules and horses.

That July, Andrew Drips and the ninety or so other American Fur Company trappers had met up at the rendezvous with the men of the Hudson's Bay Company, the Rocky Mountain Fur Company, and some independent trappers as well. According to Robert Campbell, "Sharbona" was one of the latter, one of the elite corps of independents who "trap by the skin."[33] Working for themselves, they did not have to share their profits, but in exchange for this freedom, they had to forego the safety and benefits of belonging to an organization. Now Jean-Baptiste and fellow trapper-by-the-skin, Jim Bridger, would join the company men for the rendezvous.

All during that unusually cold spring and summer of 1832, the men had looked forward to this grand rendezvous at Pierre's Hole to warm and revive them. But this year there seemed no end to the cold as rain, snow, and hail continued into July.[34] They were determined, however, that the weather would not keep them from having a good time. At last, for these two carefree weeks, they could mingle and share sto-

---

[33] Dale I. Morgan and Eleanor Towles Harris, eds., *The Rocky Mountain Journals of William Marshall Anderson*, 284.   [34] Fred R. Gowans, *Rocky Mountain Rendezvous*, 65.

ries, shaking off the loneliness of the long wilderness winter. In general, except for the American Fur Company and the Rocky Mountain Fur Company, who chose to camp in separate areas, bad feelings between the companies did not carry over into these festive times. Here the fierce competition shifted to pranks and games of sport. Amazing exhibitions of horsemanship, wrestling, and feats of strength thrilled all who watched, until the whiskey took over and the scene degenerated into the antics of the "crazy drunk."[35]

Eager to get this rendezvous underway, the men of the American Fur Company anxiously awaited the arrival of Lucien Fontenelle from the East and Etienne Provost from Fort Union with all of their provisions for the new season. Their anxiety increased on July 8 when William Sublette and Thomas Fitzpatrick arrived with about one hundred mules laden with Rocky Mountain Fur Company supplies, but there was still no sign of Fontenelle and Provost.[36] The trappers feared the worst when they heard of Fitzpatrick's near brush with death on the trail. He had been attacked by Indians and wandered lost for ten days. Miraculously, he had been saved just in time, and he and Sublette were feeling lucky. But luck had deserted the American Fur Company. Their provisioners never did arrive, and it would be a difficult season ahead for the employees.

Trading and other rendezvous activities continued for several days, and then the brigades assembled to head out for the fall trapping season. Although it was the American Fur Company that had suffered bad luck at the rendezvous, danger now shifted to its rival, the Rocky Mountain Fur Company. Milton Sublette, brother of William, joined his brigade of about thirty men to another group of about thirty more as

---

[35]Joe Meek in Victor, *The River of the West*, 110–11.
[36]Paul C. Phillips, ed., *W. A. Ferris, Life in the Rocky Mountains*, 152.

they headed out on the July 18. Soon they saw a large group approaching from afar. Was it Fontenelle and Provost at long last? As the band came nearer, the truth became unpleasantly evident. It was a large party of Atsena, the allies of the dreaded Blackfeet! Two of Milton Sublette's men initiated hostilities and soon the battle raged. Fortunately for the traders, others at the rendezvous had been alerted and they soon joined in. Warren Ferris wrote that Drips had a close call when his hat was shot through by a bullet, shearing off a lock of his hair. William Sublette was not so fortunate. He was severely injured, while fourteen others from the rendezvous, including trappers, a *métis*, and seven Nez Perce, were killed. Later on, at Jackson Hole, three more of the men, traveling in a party of seven, were killed by Blackfeet as they attempted to return to St. Louis. Among the four survivors were two grandsons of Daniel Boone.[37]

The western fur trade was indeed a dangerous business, and not just because of hostile Indians. Jean-Baptiste was about to find himself in the thick of this peril as competition between the two main companies turned lethal. William Sublette had offered to split the territory, but the American Fur Company refused, not wanting their territory limited. When the Rocky Mountain traders set out, the men of the American Fur Company were in hot pursuit. As Gowans stated, "[T]he fall hunt was a continual game of hide and seek between the two companies. The Rocky Mountain Fur Company had the knowledge of the land and the expertise in trapping, but the American Fur Company had the money and the time to make life miserable for its competitor."[38] Among the most savvy trappers was Jean-Baptiste's companion that year, Jim Bridger. This legendary Mountain

---

[37] Washington Irving, *Captain Bonneville*, 48, 54.
[38] Gowans, *Rocky Mountain Rendezvous*, 78–79.

Man and discoverer of the Great Salt Lake found himself dogged by American Fur Trade men wherever he went. He tried everything to get the followers off his tail so he could begin his season in peace. One desperate measure was to stray dangerously close to Blackfeet lands. Still, he was not able to shake the likes of William Vanderburgh, Alexis Pillon, and Andrew Drips. One time, after Bridger had moved safely on, these pursuers found themselves caught up in an Indian attack. By the time it was over, both Vanderburgh and Pillon lie dead. Even Bridger could not always escape the dangers of Blackfeet territory. Later, he too encountered some Indians and let his guard down when they appeared to be friendly, only to receive two arrows in his back. Fortunately, both missed vital organs. One was pulled out right away, but the other had to await surgical intervention by a preacher three years later.

If Jean-Baptiste was with Bridger when he was injured, there is no mention of it. But we do know that the two young men were working together that summer in the Laramie Mountains. With similar abilities and just a year apart in age, it is not surprising that these two St. Louis-bred men paired up. Nathaniel Wyeth's journal places Jean-Baptiste in the company of Jim Bridger and Henry Fraeb that summer after the breakup of the rendezvous. Wyeth, another independent trapper, was traveling with Fitzpatrick's brigade to the Big Horn, where he mentioned seeing Jean-Baptiste on July 31, 1832. Wyeth had reached Beaver Creek near the Popo Agie when he encountered

> ... a party of 4 whites who have lost their horses ... one of them wounded in the head with a Ball and in the body with an arrow very badly. ... The case was this. Mr. Bridger sent 4 men to this river to look for us viz Mr. Smith, Thomson, Charboneau a half breed and Evans. Two days before it happened 15 Inds came to them (Snakes) and after smoking departed ... the second day after

they were gone Thomson [while out hunting was attacked and wounded] . . . the Inds got 7 horses all there were. Charboneau pursued them on foot but wet his gun in crossing a little stream and only snapped twice.[39]

This had been another close call for Jean-Baptiste. His associate, Thomson, had been gravely injured by a shot to the head and an arrow wound to the body. It was just as well that Jean-Baptiste had not caught up with those fifteen Indians—alone and on foot with a wet gun. He must have been mighty angry to find himself and his three companions without even one horse among them. Fortunately, Bridger and Fraeb were able to accommodate their horseless companions, and they all set out together once again to the wild lands of southwest Idaho. They parted with Wyeth near the junction of the Snake and Owyhee Rivers.[40]

1833 at Green River and the Yellowstone

In the spring of 1833, the American Fur Company played host to royalty. Prince Maximilian of Wied-Neuwied had arrived in St. Louis with the excellent, young artist, Karl Bodmer. After getting the requisite permits from William Clark, they had boarded the American Fur Company's steamboat *Yellowstone,* bound for the upper Missouri. Like his fellow Germanic noblemen, Paul of Württemberg and Alexander von Humboldt, Maximilian had been swept up in the Enlightenment pursuits of natural history and ethnogra-

---

[39] A. W. Hafen, "Jean-Baptiste Charbonneau," 84; "The Correspondence and Journals of Captain Nathaniel J. Wyeth, 1831–6," in *Sources of the History of Oregon*, I: 207; Morgan and Harris, eds. (*The Rocky Mountain Journals of William Marshall Anderson*, 284–5), cite Robert Campbell's journal as to "Sharbona" working as an independent trapper in 1832, but they have the encounter with Wyeth taking place in 1833. Wyeth's journal, on the other hand, clearly indicates the encounter took place in 1832.

[40] William R. Sampson, "Nathaniel Jarvis Wyeth," 318; two years later it would be Kit Carson who was injured in an unsuccessful attempt to recover fifteen of Bridger's stolen horses. See Victor, *The River of the West.*

phy. His interpreter for several months of this journey would be none other than Toussaint Charbonneau, who also assisted the prince with his ethnographic and linguistic studies. The prince, age fifty-one, a veteran of several Prussian wars and prior field studies in Brazil, respected the abilities of sixty-six-year-old Toussaint and his thirty-seven years of experience with the Hidatsa people. On one occasion, Toussaint intervened to save Prince Maximilian, who had enraged a warrior by refusing to surrender his pocket compass. The prince wrote afterwards in his journal that "it was only by the assistance of old Charbonneau, that I escaped a disagreeable and, perhaps, violent scene."[41] Toussaint provided many other services throughout the following winter and was commended by the prince for his "patience and kindness."[42]

Meanwhile, that same summer, Toussaint's son remained, as usual, further west. According to Howard,[43] Jean-Baptiste did attend that first, great Green River rendezvous, and we can only hope that he was indeed a part of that memorable scene. The beautiful Green River valley, near present-day Daniel, Wyoming, was to become the preferred site in years to come, hosting the rendezvous for five out of the next seven years. This year was special, though. According to Sir William Drummond Stewart, it was "the last good year, for with 1834 came the spoilers—the idlers, the missionaries, the hard seekers after money."[44] The times were changing—settlers were coming and the furs were playing out, but for this special year, spirits were high and life as a Mountain Man was at its height.

---

[41]Thwaites, "Maximilian, Prince of Weid," 22: 350–51.
[42]Ibid., 254–55, n.212; Schierle, ed., *Travels in the Interior of North America*, 27, 30.
[43]Harold P. Howard (*Sacajawea*, 172) places Jean-Baptiste at the Green River rendezvous in 1833, but Morgan and Harris, eds. (*The Rocky Mountain Journals of William Marshall Anderson*, 284–85) say he and Bridger did not attend it. Morgan and Harris's confusion of 1832 and 1833 may be the reason they rule out Jean-Baptiste's presence at the 1833 rendezvous. [44]Gowans, *Rocky Mountain Rendezvous*, 96.

After the fur traders settled in, the first provisioner they saw was William Sublette, now heading the re-organized Rocky Mountain Fur Company/St. Louis Fur Company. Fontenelle and Drips of the American Fur Company followed just three days later on July 8. Still wary of one another, the two companies camped four or five miles apart. Also joining the competition that year was Captain Bonneville's crew. Tragedy soon struck the camps when rabid dogs and wolves attacked, and several men died agonizing deaths. These hardships brought the 250 to 300 men of the various camps together. Regardless of the ill will between their companies, they were all cut from the same cloth, and they were drawn together for safety, games, tall tales, and the camaraderie and support shared only by men who admire one another. Soon the shooting, riding, running, jumping, and wrestling rivalries were in full swing, followed by much feasting and carousing. Many pipes full of the traditional mixture of tobacco and *shongsasha* (red cedar bark) were passed around. "They drank together, they sang, they laughed, they whooped; they tried to out-brag and out-lie each other in stories of their adventures and achievements . . . but it all ended in cordial reconsiliation [*sic*] and maudlin endearment."[45]

A great many Indians were in attendance as well. And many a trapper tried to make himself presentable and his trade items tempting to the young Shoshoni maidens. Soon their hard-earned pay was squandered and the men were ready to return to their lonely traps in the mountains. Although they used the rendezvous to shed their cares and kick up their heels, they were not out of control, as Wyeth informed Hudson's Bay's F. Ermatinger: "I should have been proud of my countrymen if you could have seen the Ameri-

---

[45]Irving, *The Adventures of Captain Bonneville*, 180–183.

Trapper's Bride, by Alfred Jacob Miller. Courtesy The Walters Art Museum, Baltimore.

can Fur Co. or the party of Mr. S. Campbell. For efficiency of goods, men, animals, and arms, I do not believe the fur business has afforded a better example of discipline."[46]

Late that summer, Jean-Baptiste traveled to the Yellowstone River, either by bull boat with Robert Campbell or by land with Louis Vasquez, arriving by September 3. Campbell recorded that on September 26, 1833, he sent Jean-Baptiste to Fitzpatrick; and on December 22, the Crows told Kenneth Mackenzie that Jean-Baptiste had been with them. He probably continued south to intersect with Fitzpatrick, in whose camp he was seen the following June and August.[47]

---
[46]Ibid., 72–73.
[47]Morgan and Harris, eds., *The Rocky Mountain Journals of William Marshall Anderson*, 285.

1834 and Change is in the Air

By the end of the 1833 trapping season, it was apparent that the great competition between the American Fur Company and the Rocky Mountain Fur Company was over. Better funding had won the field for the former and soon both companies would be one. William Sublette had agreed to bow out if the American Fur Company would let him have one last good year. An agreement was reached and it was William Sublette's Rocky Mountain Fur Company that supplied the traders at the 1834 rendezvous at Ham's Fork. Then Drips and Fontenelle joined up with Bridger, Fizpatrick, and Milton Sublette in August 1834 to absorb the Rocky Mountain Fur Company within the new Fontenelle, Fitzpatrick & Company.

William Marshall Anderson's journal and diary place Jean-Baptiste in Fitzpatrick's camp that summer of 1834. In his diary entry for June 23, he described Jean-Baptiste's Indian side:

> A Mock war dance was held also in Mr Fitzpatrick's camp in compliment, I believe, to me. Baptiste Charboneau, a half breed, & born of the squaw mentioned by Clark & Lewis, on their journey, was the principal actor in this scene. Of which there is something whispered which makes him an object of much interest to me. At all events he is an intelligent and interesting young man. He converses fluently & well in English, reading & writing & speaking with ease French and German—understan[din]g several of the Indian dialects—[48]

Anderson's journal entry for the same date added a few more facts. The dance was performed by two or three *métis* and several young Indians with Jean-Baptiste as the "principal actor in this scenic representation—To me it was a very agreeable spectacle—." Another recorder of that day, Jason Lee,

---
[48] Ibid., 142–43. See footnote as to Jason Lee.

mentioned that, after dark that night, three *métis* preformed the war dance around a fire after the whites had made fools of themselves trying to do the dance. Since Jean-Baptiste had taken the time to learn the dance properly, performing it respectfully and without embarrassment before the white men, it is clear that he was proud of his Indian heritage.

A darker side of Jean-Baptiste's personality emerged a few weeks later. On August 5, 1834, W. M. Anderson's diary recorded a scene of violence in the camp of Drips and Fontenelle: "Young Charbonneau stuck his butcher knife into a fellow for wishing to flog him, for merely telling him that he was a rogue."

In his journal, Anderson provided more details:

> A stabbing match took place, which has like to have produced serious disturbances in both camps. Last night—horses were cut loose and halters were stolen, which led this morning to the charges and recriminations that produced the difficulty—Charbonneau accused a young white fellow whom he had discovered prowling about in the night with having committed the theft—for which compliment he was kind enough to offer Baptiste a flogging—not choosing it, and being somewhat liberally inclined he lent the accused his butcher-knife up to the hilt in the muscles of his shoulder—[49]

Frontier justice was the only justice. A man who would not or could not stand up to thieves, bullies, bigots, and hooligans would not last long. Perhaps Jean-Baptiste was also sending the message that, although he was a "half-breed," no white man should entertain the thought that he had the right to flog him. A bold demeanor was also required in the presence of Indians. Many a westbound traveler was disposed of promptly and with contempt for lack of a self-confident bearing.[50]

The editors of W. M. Anderson's journals add that Ander-

---
[49] Ibid., 174–75.
[50] Parkman, *The Oregon Trail*, 93.

son did not mention Jean-Baptiste again for five years. Perhaps this signals Jean-Baptiste's abandonment of Upper Missouri trapping for the Santa Fe Trail. Anderson's entry for the very next day, August 6, 1834, stated that Bridger and Carson and fifty other men left Anderson's party that day to begin their fur-trapping season. If Jean-Baptiste were with them, he may well have accompanied them to the Southwest the following season. But first, there was danger on the trail. Kit Carson recorded that, as they passed through Blackfeet territory, five of their men were killed, and a trapper could hardly go a mile without being fired upon. There was no hope for it but to head for winter quarters. They reached the Big Snake River by November and settled in until February.[51] Bridger then went down to assess possibilities in the Spanish Southwest, and this soon became the new focus for many savvy fur-traders, including Jean-Baptiste Charbonneau. We lose sight of Jean-Baptiste during the following five years, however, as there are no well-documented references to his activities.[52] In the summer of 1839, however, he is well-established on the Santa Fe Trail.

---

[51] Morgan and Harris, eds., *The Rocky Mountain Journals of William Marshall Anderson*, 174 and note for August 6; DeVoto (*Across the Wide Missouri*, 378) reports Bridger in the Southwest.

[52] According to Peabody ("'Pomp' is First Baby Ever on a U.S. Coin"), Jean-Baptist was with William F. May in August 1837 among the Gros Ventres, where smallpox was raging. It is clear, however, that Peabody confused Jean-Baptiste with his father; see L. R. Hafen, ed. (*The Mountain Men and the Fur Trade of the Far West*, 9: 61), who noted that on September 6, 1837, an Indian wife of Toussaint died of smallpox there. Toussaint's boss, Chardon, mentioned Toussaint often in his journals during the 1830s but never mentioned the son being present. This confusion of father with son may also account for Carl Waldman's (*Biographical Dictionary*, 65) comment that "with the decline of the Rocky Mountain fur trade in the 1830s, Charbonneau [meaning Jean-Baptiste] turned to guiding explorers on the Upper Missouri River." He did do this but not until the mid-1840s.

Chapter Six

The Spanish Southwest

There is a spirit of energy in mountains, and they impart it to all who approach them.
— *Francis Parkman, 1846*[1]

Bent's Fort and the Santa Fe Trail

Doom was threatening the Upper Missouri fur enterprise by 1835. Demand for beaver pelts was dwindling. Supply was scarcer as well, as too many trappers had cleared too much territory of beaver. The rendezvous at Green River would be less joyous this year. The revelries were also dampened by the presence of missionaries, the inevitable forerunners of settlers and their civilization. Ironically, it was the traders themselves who had facilitated this civilizing trend. Lucien Fontenelle and the American Fur Company had brought missionary Dr. Marcus Whitman with them that summer to establish the first mission on the Columbia River. Some, like Jim Bridger, who had returned from the Spanish Southwest for the rendezvous, appreciated Dr. Whitman's medical abilities more than his ministerial skills: The good doctor provided the service of removing the three-inch iron arrowhead that had been embedded in Bridger's back since his run-in with the Blackfeet in 1832.

Santa Fe had long attracted the adventurous. Toussaint

---
[1]Parkman, *The Oregon Trail*, 134.

may have spent some time there as early as 1815.[2] If so, soon his son would follow his trail. Now that the Northwest was being tamed, Jean-Baptiste and many other mountain men felt the time was right to abandon the northern Rockies for trade along the Santa Fe Trail. The hub of much of this activity was Bent's Fort on the Arkansas River (near La Junta in present-day southeastern Colorado). Rather than beaver pelts, Bent's Fort focused on buffalo robes and facilitating trade between St. Louis and New Mexico. It was in an excellent location for trade with several tribes, including Cheyennes, Arapahoes, Mountain Utes, Jicarills, and Apaches. This well-built fort had been finished in 1834 by three St. Louis men who enjoyed the respect of both the white men and the tribes: Ceran St. Vrain and the Bent brothers, William and Charles, the sons of Judge Silas Bent. No doubt Jean-Baptiste had known them in St. Louis. Perhaps he had been acquainted with St. Vrain, who was just three years his senior, from their school days. A contemporary, Lewis H. Garrard, described St. Vrain as

> a gentleman in the true sense of the term, his French descent imparting an exquisite, indefinable degree of politeness . . . [which] combined with the frankness of a mountain man, made him an amiable fellow traveler. His kindness and respect for me, I shall always gratefully remember.[3]

Like Jean-Baptiste, these educated gentlemen were also comfortable in the company of Indians, Spaniards, and English-Americans, treating all whom they met with polite respect. Likewise, the brothers Bent were decent, capable employers and companions, and Charles Bent went on to be

---

[2]Speck, *Breeds and Half-Breeds*, 122–25; L. R. Hafen, ed. (*The Mountain Men and the Fur Trade of the Far West*, 9: 59), writes of the imprisonment—some in irons—of several men in the employ of Julius McMun. This party, believed to include Toussaint, was held by the Spaniards for forty-eight days in 1815.

[3]Henry Inman, *Stories of the Old Santa Fe Trail*, 124–32.

selected governor of New Mexico. It is no wonder that Jean-Baptiste chose to remain in the employ of these fine men for several years, especially since the Bents were on excellent terms with his former employers at the American Fur Company.[4]

Bent's Fort was the only permanent white settlement on the Santa Fe Trail between Missouri and the Mexican settlements. It was, therefore, a very important collection and dispersal point for all manner of goods and travelers—fur traders, Indians, merchants, explorers, and military expeditions—throughout the entire Southwest, and it was a big money maker for the St. Louis merchants. An imposing castle-like adobe structure of 180 by 135 feet with walls three feet thick, Bent's Fort was an oasis of luxury in the wilderness. It even sported a billiard table covered in green baize, a bar serving "Taos Lightning," an ice house with plenty of ice for the long, hot summers, and the fine cuisine of Charlotte, the black cook.[5] Such style must have appealed to the debonair Jean-Baptiste, whose educated palate, pampered in the courts of Europe for six years, suffered mightily at times on the range. Soon St. Vrain and the Bent brothers had built "the largest and strongest merchandising and fur-trading firm in the Southwest during the middle nineteenth century."[6]

Meanwhile, back in St. Louis, the boom continued. During the first five years of the 1830s, its population had doubled to twelve thousand souls. It was evolving away from its French roots into a very American city. Indians still visited Clark as they always had, including Chief Black Eagle of the Nez Perce and the Flatheads' Man of the Morning, and Clark still dazzled travelers with his private museum of western artifacts and natural history specimens, but the old days

---

[4]Harold H. Dunham, "Ceran St. Vrain," 157.   [5]David Dary, *The Santa Fe Trail*, 144.
[6]Ibid., 138–39.

were gone. The fur trade was no longer the main focus of its citizens or of its new arrivals; many were thinking instead of the settlement of the West. But there was still a lot of money to be made from the Santa Fe trade. Mexico had riches from its silver mines and it hungered for American goods. Traders from St. Louis were happy to oblige them and Clark still actively encouraged his friends in these activities. The Bent brothers were just the sort of businessmen that he wanted to encourage, as were Ceran St. Vrain and his brother Marcellin. Through their efforts and those of like-minded merchants, as well as through the hard work of their hunters and traders, who were still mainly French-Canadian, the prosperity of St. Louis was rising to new heights.[7]

Fort Vasquez (1839–1840)

In the summer of 1839, E. Willard Smith's journal placed Jean-Baptiste in the company of Louis Vasquez, Andrew Sublette, and about thirty-two of their men and four mule-drawn carts on their way to Fort Vasquez—northeast of present-day Denver—on the South Fork of the Platte River. Smith had been traveling west with this party of experienced traders out of Independence, Missouri. On August 15, 1839, he wrote that the party included "two half breeds employed as hunters. One of them (Shabenare) was a son of Captain Clarke, the great Western traveler and companion of Lewis. He had received an education in Europe during seven years."[8]

It is curious that Smith identified Jean-Baptiste as a son of Clark (with an Indian mother) but with a different last

---
[7] Faherty, *The Saint Louis Portrait*, 59.
[8] E. Willard Smith, "Journal," 254; also see L. R. and A. W. Hafen, eds., *To the Rockies and Oregon*, 155–56; Harold P. Howard, *Sacajawea*, 172; A. W. Hafen, "Jean-Baptiste Charbonneau," 85.

name. The father-son relationship had been accepted without an actual biological tie. Whoever it was who identified Jean-Baptiste for Smith (whether it was one of the others in the party or Jean-Baptiste himself) valued his close relationship with Captain Clark as well as his education abroad—even now, some thirty-four years after the Corps of Discovery's journey. This suggests that Clark's role in Jean-Baptiste's life went well beyond placing him in a school and paying the bills. These biographical details would have been lost if Jean-Baptiste had not kept them alive. We can surmise that, although Jean-Baptiste was living the life of a part-Indian hunter, he did not regret his upbringing and education in white society as a "son" of William Clark. He was a man of both worlds with no need to repudiate either or defend his choices.

Smith described the sights along the way—the herds of antelope, the bellowing buffalo, the howling wolves. There were plenty of hunting opportunities for Jean-Baptiste. The great herds of buffalo still roamed the prairies, and they could be taken by horse (called "running") or by stalking afoot (called "approaching"). As the hunters rode through the ocean of grass as high as their horses' bellies, they kept their eyes peeled for specks of black in the distance, which they hoped would prove to be bison herds and not Pawnee warriors. Leaping antelopes and prowling wolves sometimes caught their eyes, as well, as they scanned the horizon. Spotting their prey at last, Smith watched the hunters employ the "running" technique, checking the wind, then whipping their horses and flying through the grass and across the sandy hills until a clear shot at a vital spot was possible. Shooting these huge beasts randomly had no effect since their hides were so thick, but a skilled hunter could drop a buffalo from a distance of 150 yards or more. Then the swift,

Buffalo Chase, a Single Death, by George Catlin.
Accession number 1985-66.408. Smithsonian American
Art Museum, Gift of Mrs. Joseph Harrison, Jr.

expert butchering would begin, and the successful hunter could claim the hide and the tongue, strapping the other choice cuts to his horse for the others.[9] When the pursuit was for commercial purposes, hunters like Jean-Baptiste preferentially sought female buffalos since their finer pelts made better blankets and hides. This mid-August prey, however, was better suited for meat since buffalos molt in the spring, and the best time to take their hides is late fall through winter.[10]

---

[9]Parkman (*The Oregon Trail*, 57–69, 177–78, 282–304) describes the art and skill of buffalo hunting and butchering. [10]Ibid., 294, 311.

Eventually, Smith's party reached the South Fork of the Platte, trading the endless grasses for the endless sands, bisected by this mile-wide, shallow river. Dropping down to the Arkansas, Bent's Fort soon loomed into view like a mirage, its high clay walls visible for miles over the scorched, flat terrain. The pace quickened as the men anticipated the comforts promised by this oasis.

Two other references to Jean-Baptiste that year are less reliable: first, according to Campbell, Kit Carson and his men had joined E. Willard Smith's party, and on October 2, 1839, "Chabonard" had enjoyed telling Kit's men his Indian stories;[11] and second, Jean-Baptiste could have been that educated Indian with whom Farnham conversed that year at Fort El Pueblo near Bent's Fort, but there is no corroboration for it.[12]

After spending fall through spring hunting in the vicinity of Fort Vasquez, Jean-Baptiste was ready to take the furs east on April 26, 1840. With six other men he loaded up a mackinaw boat for the long journey east on the South Platte. This boat, about the same size as the 1805 pirogue of his first journey, carried a heavy load—seven hundred buffalo robes and four hundred tongues. They were lucky this year because, for most of the journey, they found the river deep enough to float the 36-foot-long by 8-foot-wide boat laden with buffalo products. Even so, they still got stuck on the sand bars from time to time over the 300-mile journey. This tedious trip took forty-nine days. To lighten the load and

---

[11] Harold P. Howard, *Sacajawea*, 172, cites Walter S. Campbell's *Kit Carson*, but Harvey L. Carter ("Kit Carson," 176 n.23) states that Campbell (a.k.a. Stanley Vestal) and others were duped in many regards by William F. Drannan (*Thirty-one Years on the Plains and in the Mountains*, 1900), who has since been exposed as a fraud.

[12] Thwaites, ed., "Farnham, Farnham's Travels," 28: 176, 179; see Chapter 5 herein for the full quote. Since the "educated Indian" is not named, it remains fanciful, as Furtwangler ("Sacagawea's Son as a Symbol," 309–10) points out, to assume he is Jean-Baptiste, but see chapter 5, note 18 herein.

feed the men, all four hundred tongues were consumed on the way, but Jean-Baptiste procured more meat when he could. Smith was still with the party and wrote of one of Jean-Baptiste's hunting forays:

> This afternoon we had, as usual, tied up our boat, and the hunter, Mr. Shabenare, went out a short distance from the river bank to shoot a buffalo for his meat. At the time there were several large buffalo bulls near us. After killing one we assisted the hunters in butchering it, and in carrying portions of the meat to the boat.[13]

Here Jean-Baptiste used the "approaching" method for hunting buffalo on foot. This technique required a stealthy approach. The hunter had to be "cool, collected, and watchful; must understand the buffalo, observe the features of the country and the course of the wind, and be well skilled in using the rifle."[14] Sometimes this proved surprisingly easy but at other times it was highly dangerous and required great skill. The rest of the trip went well and the party successfully arrived in St. Louis just in time for the 1840 Independence Day celebrations.

1841 & 1842—Mint Juleps on the Platte

Two years later, Jean-Baptiste was not so fortunate. As so often happened on the South Fork of the Platte River in summer, the water was too low in 1842 to float the furs to market. Jean-Baptiste, still in the employ of Bent and St. Vrain, understood the problem well and did not let it frustrate him. He established himself and his hired men in a comfortable camp and entertained those passing through with fine food, style, and wit. Among those who visited Jean-Baptiste's Platte River camp that summer was his old friend, Jim Beckwourth, with his Spanish bride, Louisa

---

[13] E. Willard Smith, "Journal," 277; also see L. R. and A. W. Hafen, eds., *To the Rockies and Oregon*, 192–193, and A. W. Hafen, "Jean-Baptiste Charbonneau," 85–86.
[14] Parkman, *The Oregon Trail*, 284.

Sandoval.[15] Soon they were joined by John C. Frémont and his guide Kit Carson, who were on their historic expedition of exploration for the United States Topographical Bureau.

It was July 9, 1842, and the Frémont expedition was on its way to the Rockies, now visible for the first time about sixty miles off in the distance. Frémont's party approached the camp and was delighted with their reception. "Mr. C. received us hospitably," commented Frémont, and he added that they were then presented with mint juleps and such delicacies as boiled buffalo tongue and coffee with sugar, a true rarity in those parts.[16] Frémont and Carson spent a pleasant day with Jean-Baptiste on his island in the Platte, which he had dubbed "St. Helena." Here is another insight into Jean-Baptiste's wit, which reflects his education and ironic sense of humor—Jean-Baptiste had named his own little "island of exile" for that of Napoleon. Recalling Clark's "Pompy's Tower," the source of Jean-Baptiste's sense of humor becomes evident.

What a colorful party that must have been, and what adventurous stories must have been told by the rough-and-ready black trader (and former Crow chief), Beckwourth, the savvy guides, Charbonneau and Carson, and the intrepid Franco-American, Frémont! Frémont recognized Beckwourth's wife as a Spanish woman from Taos and he added that Jean-Baptiste generally had Spaniards in his employ. One wonders what language they used for their conversations on that memorable summer's day—did they switch as needed from French to English to Spanish? Perhaps it was the gentle Spanish conversation of Beckwourth's bride that inspired Carson to take the plunge himself. He, too, found a

[15]Bonner, *The Life and Adventures of James P. Beckwourth*, 586; according to Michael S. Durham (*Desert Between the Mountains*, 39), Beckwourth had many wives among the Indians as well, including Blackfoot, Snake, and Crow women.
[16]Frémont, *Report of the Exploring Expedition to the Rocky Mountains*, 31.

bride in Taos the following February. As far as we know, however, our Jean-Baptiste remained impervious to such tender traps. There is a tantalizing hint of a wife, however, in the December 28, 1847, entry of Alexander Barclay's diary, alluding to a possible Cheyenne wife. At Pueblo, Barclay ran into a Mountain Man who said he had "met Rufine and Charbonneaus child Louise at the Whirlwinds camp going down to Bents fort alone and afoot." Others propose that Jean-Baptiste took a French-Canadian bride in 1834 or in 1842 and fathered a child who was born in Montreal in 1843, but genealogical research does not support these claims.[17]

---

[17]Morgan and Harris, eds., *The Rocky Mountain Journals of William Marshall Anderson*, 288. If this Cheyenne child were old enough to travel alone, she was probably at least twelve, and so she might have been born soon after Jean-Baptiste started trading in Cheyenne country in the mid-1830s. However, since neither Rufine nor Louise is mentioned anywhere else, we cannot know if this is a valid reference. Also, Richard Scheuerman, personal communication, interviewed a Tom Sharbono and others in Coeur d'Alene, Idaho, who believed Tom to be a direct descendent of Jean-Baptiste Charbonneau and a Charlotte Guery. They say Jean-Baptiste returned to St. Louis in 1842 and married Charlotte. She bore him a son, Joseph, the following year in Montreal. Genealogical research, however, reveals contradictory information, none of which supports Sharbono's claim. The following is on record with the Charbonneau Association in Quebec: First, on January 31, 1813, a Jean-Baptiste Charbonneau married a Charlotte Dumont-Query (Guery) at St. Henri de Mascouche, Quebec, but this is not the son of Toussaint. (Since Toussaint's Jean-Baptiste was born in 1805, he cannot be the Jean-Baptiste who married in 1813.) Second, on November 24, 1833, another Jean-Baptiste Charbonneau married Louise Boucher at St. Boniface, Manitoba. This Jean-Baptiste Charbonneau was the son of Joseph Charbonneau and Marguerite Lamoureux, and he is definitely not Toussaint's son. (See Nute, *The Voyageur*, 218–221, for his story.) Third, the Charbonneau Association does believe that Jean-Baptiste Charbonneau, son of Toussaint, did marry a Charlotte Dumont-Query (Guery) in 1834 at St. Boniface, Manitoba, but they have no proof. They referred me to St. Boniface, where I consulted researcher Les W. Branconnier. He searched all files and found no marriage for a Jean-Baptiste Charbonneau who was the son of Toussaint; he found only the November 24, 1833, marriage cited above between a Jean-Baptiste Charbonneau, son of Joseph Charbonneau and Louise Boucher. In sum, we have two Charlotte Querys (Guery) marrying Jean-Baptistes, in 1813 and in 1834, neither of which is the couple Tom Sharbono has marrying in 1842 in St. Louis. Further, I have reviewed papers on file at the Auburn Placer County Library titled "History of the Charbonneau (Sharbono) Families. Descendents of Oliver Charbonneau and Marie Marguerite Garnier, Morans France," provided to the library by Tom Sharbono, which show a marriage of Jean-Baptiste Charbonneau and Charlotte Dumont Guery on October 10, 1842, in St. Louis, Missouri, "St. Esprit Country." If this should read St. Esprit *County*, it cannot refer to St. Louis, Missouri, as St. Louis is in St. Louis County. Jean-Baptiste is referred to as "Jean

The following month, on August 30, 1842, Mountain Man Rufus Sage, who had run into Jean-Baptiste on the White River in 1841, encountered him again at this same camp on the South Platte. In his journals Sage often wrote in a condescending manner about French-Canadians and *métis*, but he was clearly awed by this encounter:

> The company was under the direction of a half-breed, named Chabonard, who proved to be a gentleman of superior information. He had acquired a classic education and could converse quite fluently in German, Spanish, French, and English, as well as several Indian languages. His mind, also, was well stored with choice reading, and enriched by extensive travel and observation. Having visited most of the important places, both in England, France, and Germany, he knew how to turn his experience to good advantage.
>
> There was a quaint humor and shrewdness in his conversation, so garbed with intelligence and perspicuity, that he at once insinuated himself into the good graces of listeners, and commanded their admiration and respect.[18]

1843—Sentimental Journeys

The Santa Fe Trail was closed in 1843 because of the rebellion in Texas, but Jean-Baptiste was not idle. He stepped into his father's shoes by assisting the rich and famous on a tour of the West. Ten years after Toussaint had interpreted for the Scotsman Sir William Drummond Steward, Jean-Baptiste was hired by William Sublette to assist another Steward party on a westward expedition. That spring he joined the Steward party of about eighty gentleman hunters and adventure-seekers in the capacity of a hunter and cart driver. It

---

Born April 8, 1805," a date which is off by about two months. These undocumented papers with erroneous names and dates only muddy the record for the alleged Charbonneau-Guery marriage. Somehow, these records have become hopelessly entangled, but at this time no records have been found supporting any marriage by Jean-Baptiste Charbonneau, son of Toussaint and Sacagawea. In sum, claims made by Tom Sharbono were undoubtedly made in good faith but there is no supporting documentation for them and there is a lot of documentation contradicting them.

[18]Sage, *Rocky Mountain Life*, 206.

would be a six-month trip to what is now Yellowstone Park. This was rather tame employment for someone of Jean-Baptiste's abilities. Perhaps he was drawn to the project because of his loyalty to his late mentor, William Clark, and his godfather, Auguste Chouteau, for also included in the party were Clark's son, Jefferson Kennerly Clark, stepson John Radford, nephews Clark Kennerly and William Clark Kennett, and also a young Chouteau, Edmund Francis Xavier Chouteau. On the tour, as well, were the governor's son, Cyprien Menard, and some other sons of the St. Louis elite. These lads were in their teens, spirited greenhorns who might well bear some looking after. Indeed this did prove to be the case when Cyprien got lost on the trail. Fortunately, the boy had the presence of mind to write a note on a buffalo skull. Sublette followed the trail for six miles to another note and, after four desperate days, the governor's son was rescued. Another young man in the party, François Clement, just fifteen years of age, was not so fortunate; he was killed in a rifle accident.

Sublette recorded that the well-liked Clark Kennerly had a very close call as well. Still excited after witnessing his first buffalo hunt the night before, he had caught his foot in his saddle rope and it was feared he would be dragged to his death. There was great relief in camp when he was able to get back up on his feet after the incident. Later in life, Clark Kennerly commented on the ironic twist of fate that had brought the next generation of the Clark and Charbonneau families together again:

> To each six men was alloted one two-wheeled cart, or charette, the covers of which, I remember, were painted red; each cart was drawn by two mules driven tandem.
> One of the drivers, Baptiste Charbonneau, was the son of the old trapper Charbonneau and Sacajawea, the brave Indian woman who had guided Lewis and Clark on their perilous journey

through the wilderness.... By a singular coincidence he [Baptiste] was now again to make the journey and guide the *son* of William Clark through the same region.[19]

Jean-Baptiste was a young man of twenty by the time Clark's son, Jefferson Clark, had been born and they probably knew each other only slightly, but the boy's red hair and round face must have recalled the father to his mind and reminded him of his own teen-aged years with Clark. Old Sioux chiefs at Fort Laramie, where the party celebrated the Fourth of July, had this same experience. They recognized the father's face and red hair on the lad and invited him to a feast where presents were exchanged. Later, another Sioux, *O-kee-ka-gha*, became excited on seeing Clark's boy and showed him the Jefferson medal that Clark had given him about thirty-eight years before. This reunion of the sons of William Clark and Sacagawea inspired the curiosity of someone years later who asked Clark Kennerly if Jean-Baptiste had ever spoken of his mother on the trip. Replied Clark's nephew, "I regret to say that he spoke more often of the mules he was driving and might have been heard early and late expatiating in not too complimentary a manner on their stubbornness."[20]

Jean-Baptiste did not spend the entire six months with this expedition, however. By August 14, 1843, he was back in St. Louis to settle his father's affairs. Although there is no record of Toussaint's death, it is inferred by Jean-Baptiste's return at this time. Toussaint Charbonneau's long associa-

---

[19]Kennerly and Russell, *Persimmon Hill*, 144; A. W. Hafen, "Jean-Baptiste Charbonneau," 87–88. These small French carts were just like their counterparts in Quebec, but in the western U.S. they got harder use and were commonly called "mule killers" (Parkman, *The Oregon Trail*, 1, 10–11).

[20]Kennerly and Russell, *Persimmon Hill*, 144; Parkman (*The Oregon Trail*, 217, 251) explains that mules work best but they are difficult to control and will try to return home even when hobbled.

tion with William Clark had ended only with Clark's death in 1838. The old French-Canadian interpreter's steady employment on government business ended as well soon afterwards, but he still had some life left in him. Chardon described the feast Toussaint gave at Fort Clark upon yet another marriage in October 1838 to an Assiniboine girl of fourteen years![21]

Toussaint had spent 1834 to 1839 associated with Fort Clark. Besides accumulating at least three wives, he had spent those five years continuing to exercise his abilities as a trader, interpreter, and cook, earning top wages. His holiday feasts of meat pies, bread, fricasseed pheasants, boiled tongues, and roast beef had won him many friends. Like his son, he managed to avoid several brushes with death. For example, in 1836, two bullets passed through his hat without touching him. Then, in April 1838, many assumed his long-standing nightmare of drowning had finally been realized. He was missing for several days after his canoe with six hundred robes overturned and was lost. Somehow the old man survived, returning to camp by canoe a week later along with four hundred of the robes. The last recorded report of him was in August 1839, when he visited the office of the superintendent of Indian Affairs to collect his wages, only to learn that his services had been terminated six months previously. Sadly, so many Hidatsas had died in the 1837 smallpox epidemic that a Hidatsa interpreter was no longer needed.[22]

---

[21] DeVoto, *Across the Wide Missouri*, 134; Abel (*F. A. Chardon, Chardon's Journal at Fort Clark*, 173) details Toussaint's activities at Fort Clark from 1834 to 1839, including the acquisition of at least three wives.

[22] Olive Burt, *Sacajawea*, 51. According to Drumm (*Journal of a Fur-Trading Expedition on the Upper Missouri*, 140), Lean Wolf, a Hidatsa, reported that Toussaint himself lost family in that 1837 epidemic, when his daughter or granddaughter died. Abel (*F.A. Chardon, Chardon's Journal at Fort Clark*, entry for October 22, 1834) says that Toussaint's wife died September 6, 1837, in the epidemic. According to Prince Maximilian (Schierle, ed., *Travels in the Interior of North America*), 90 percent of the Mandans died in the 1837 smallpox epidemic.

The tired old man collected his pay and disappeared back into the woods, never to be mentioned in records or journals again. Most historians agree Toussaint must have died about 1843 since that is when Jean-Baptiste settled his father's affairs, selling some land for $320.[23] If this is true, the old trapper-interpreter-guide died at about the age of seventy-six. Both of Jean-Baptiste's fathers were gone now, as were all of his ties to St. Louis. He was soon seeking a way to return to the West for good.

1844—Back on the Santa Fe Trail

Having had his fill of wrangling stubborn mules and babysitting greenhorns, Jean-Baptiste was relieved to hear of the reopening of the Santa Fe Trail on March 31, 1844, just in time for provisioning a new season. Soon afterwards, he was headed west with Solomon Sublette who, on June 6, wrote from the South Platte to his brother William that he was being assisted by "M. St. Vrain Ward & Shavano."[24] Their venture was to hunt antelope and bighorn sheep, capturing them alive for Sir William Drummond Stewart's estate in Scotland. No doubt this project had been discussed over many a campfire during the previous summer.

It was at Bent's fort that winter that William M. Boggs, son of the governor of Missouri, encountered him:

---

[23]Promissory note dated August 17, 1843, in the Sublette Papers, Missouri Historical Society: "I promise to pay to J. B. Charbonno the Sum of Three hundred and twenty dollars, as soon as I dispose of land Claimed by him said Chabonno from the estate of his Deceased Father."—dated and signed J. B. Charbonneau: "To be paid W.A. Sublette." (Was this the 320 acres—worth one dollar an acre?—that Toussaint was given as a bonus for his work with the Corps of Discovery?) A claim by Jacques Vaillancourt ("Sacagawea 1790–1812," 39) that Toussaint died February 19, 1852, in Richewood, Missouri, has since been retracted (personal communication with Vaillancourt).

[24]Morgan and Harris, eds., *The Rocky Mountain Journals of William Marshall Anderson*, 286; Letters of Solomon Sublette, Sublette Collection, Missouri Historical Society. "Ward" is Seth E. Ward, chief trader at Fort St. Vrain.

I also learned considerable from the hunters of Bent's Fort, particularly from Charbenau, an educated half-breed. His father was a French Canadian, his mother said to be a Blackfoot Indian squaw. . . . This Baptiste Charbenau, the hunter of Bent's Fort, was the small Indian papoose, or half-breed of the elder Charbenau that was employed by the Lewis and Clark Expedition as guide when they descended the Columbia River to the Pacific Ocean. He had been educated to some extent; he wore his hair long—that hung down to his shoulders. It was said that Charbenau was the best man on foot on the plains or in the Rocky Mountains.[25]

1845—Trail Blazing for the War with Mexico

The following year brought a reunion of Jean-Baptiste and Thomas Fitzpatrick, an old competitor and fellow Mountain Man from the Upper Missouri days. Recall that Fitzpatrick was the hardy trader who had nearly perished in an 1832 Indian attack. There had been tense seasons in the 1830s when Jean-Baptiste, associated with the American Fur Company, had squared off against Thomas Fitzpatrick with the Rocky Mountain Fur Company. In other seasons, as in 1834, they had worked together. The comradeship of memories and mutual admiration returned now as they planned an expedition with Lieutenant James W. Abert in anticipation of the Mexican War.[26] While still at the fort on August 9, Jean-Baptiste called upon Lieutenant Abert to accompany him on a visit to an important Cheyenne chief, *Nah-co-men-si* (Winged Bear, Old Bark), who was then visiting Bent's Fort. Maintaining respectful relationships with Indian chiefs was essential for trade and for survival. But there is also that tantalizing possibility that Jean-Baptiste had a Cheyenne wife and daughter. Was he taking Abert to meet his kin?

Soon Jean-Baptiste and Thomas Fitzpatrick accompanied Lieutenant Abert and twenty-nine others (along with

---

[25]William M. Boggs Journal 1844–45 in Harold P. Howard, *Sacajawea*, 173.
[26]Morgan and Harris eds., *The Rocky Mountain Journals of William Marshall Anderson*, 286.

their four wagons and sixty-three horses) in explorations extending from Bent's Fort down to the Canadian River. Fitzpatrick rejoiced over the good choice of the able "Mr. Chabonard" as a co-guide.[27] These two excellent guides kept their eyes peeled for Comanches and other dangers as they led the train successfully to its goal.

The Mormon Battalion and the Mexican War (1846–1847)

Spring found Jean-Baptiste on the upper Arkansas River at Hardscrabble Fort where Alexander Barclay noted his arrival from Bent's Fort on March 18, 1846.[28] Summer brought Jean-Baptiste the epic adventure of the Mexican War. The idea of adding the Republic of Texas to the United States had been growing in popularity since the early 1840s, and a resolution to that effect had been enacted by Congress on March 1, 1845. By the end of that year, Texas was declared the twenty-eighth state. Texans agreed to the annexation, but Mexico was unwilling to surrender it without a fight. War followed in April, and soon Brigadier General Stephen Watts Kearny began preparations to take his "Army of the West" over the Santa Fe Trail to New Mexico by way of Fort Leavenworth. But more troops were needed and a peculiar, symbiotic relationship proved the answer. The Mormons needed the government's permission to establish winter quarters on Indian land in Missouri as they proceeded to their new homeland. If they would provide 500 troops for the war, Captain James Allen told them, the permits they sought would be granted. For the Mormons this was "temporal salvation," while for the army it was expediency, but it did prove to be successful to the advancement of both causes.

---

[27] A. W. Hafen, "Jean-Baptiste Charbonneau," 89 n.24, cites *Journal of Lieut. J. W. Abert from Bent's Fort to St. Louis, 1845*, in *Sen. Ex. Doc.* 438, 29th Cong., 1st sess.
[28] Morgan and Harris, eds., *The Rocky Mountain Journals of William Marshall Anderson*, 286.

Thus was born the longest infantry march ever organized within the territories of the United States. On July 21, 1846, General Kearny's Mormon Battalion with its 497 men, 80 women and children, and 2,000 mules began its legendary march, which would eventually cover over two thousand miles. Each evening for many months to come, white tents, surrounded by hundreds of grazing cattle, would spread across the landscape; then, in the morning, the Mormon drums and trumpets would again call all men and beasts back to the march. Mile after mile, the soldiers, both mounted and on foot, accompanied these long wagon trains from Missouri to the Pacific Coast of California. This curious mixture of religious and military forces would become "one of the greatest marches in history," helping to secure the vast, uncharted lands of the Southwest for the United States. This first sight of troops in full uniform, as well as great numbers of white settlers and their tamed herds, amazed the western tribes and foretold to the wise the end of an era.[29] This road to change had been laid, quite literally, by the Mormon Battalion, who had done no fighting but pioneered the wagon route to the west that very soon would be followed by so many settlers. Indeed, by 1848, Bent and St. Vrain would be ruined and their Santa Fe Trail trade would go the way of the Upper Missouri enterprises before them. The era of soldiers and settlers would swiftly replace that of Indians and Mountain Men.[30]

This vast marching horde rejoiced as it approached the only oasis of civilization in the wilderness, Bent's Fort. The horses soon denuded all the grasses for miles around as the men, women, and children of the battalion scrambled to buy up all

---

[29]Durham, *Desert Between the Mountains*, 125; also see Parkman's description, *The Oregon Trail*, 248, 320–21.
[30]Lecompte, "Pierre Chouteau, Junior," 52.

the luxuries and necessities they could pack away for leaner times to come. Then the battalion pressed on into the unbearable heat for Santa Fe and southern California.[31] General Kearny came to realize, however, that the maps he had were not reliable. He needed men who knew the country well and could blaze new trails through the seven hundred dangerous miles ahead, pocked with desiccated wastelands and mountainous broken terrain. Finding such trails for a few men on horseback would not have been difficult, but he needed trails that could accommodate all of his wagons and troops and provide adequate water and forage for his huge entourage. He soon recognized in Jean-Baptiste just the skills required for the job, and he signed him up as a guide along with three other men.

Jean-Baptiste caught up with the battalion in Albuquerque on October 24, 1846, and was assigned by General Kearny to Colonel Philip St. George Cooke.[32] The colonel was pleased with this new guide who had such an interesting family history. He appreciated the legacy of Sacagawea, commenting that Jean-Baptiste, like his mother, was skillful at hunting and guiding. He also found that, like his mother and his father forty years before, Jean-Baptiste's linguistic skills would prove to be an important asset to the mission. In this case it would be Spanish that was needed. Colonel William H. Emory was impressed when objects on a hilltop, which appeared to him to be cedars or shrubs, were readily identified by Jean-Baptiste, not only as men, but specifically as Apaches. In all, Jean-Baptiste proved himself to be "an active and useful" man.[33]

---

[31]William Y. Chalfant, *Dangerous Passage*, 17; Parkman (*Oregon Trail*, 264–65) arrived at Bent's fort in the late summer of 1846 after Kearny had passed through, and he described the scene Kearny's troops left behind.
[32]Norma B. Ricketts, *The Mormon Battalion: U.S. Army of the West*, 74.
[33]Morgan and Harris, eds., *The Rocky Mountain Journals of William Marshall Anderson*, 286.

Jean-Baptiste was often mentioned in the expedition journals as he went about his many duties, such as hunting, scouting Indians and camps, and seeking water and trails as he forged the treacherous Gila River route. For example, on November 16, he returned to White Ox Creek, New Mexico, to report finding a key pass through the mountains. For all his savvy and experience, however, Jean-Baptiste still had not developed any affection for his mules:

> Since dark Charboneaux has come in; his mule gave out, he says, and he stopped for it to rest and feed a half an hour; when going to saddle it, it kicked at him and ran off; he followed it a number of miles and finally shot it; partly I suppose from anger, and partly, as he says, to get his saddle and pistols, which he brought to camp.[34]

He would rather have dealt with grizzlies than mules, it seems. Four days later, while the troops were slowly crossing the Continental Divide along the mountain pass that Jean-Baptiste had found for them, Cooke wrote in his journal:

> I discovered Charboneaux near the summit in pursuit of bears. I saw three of them up among the rocks, whilst the bold hunter was gradually nearing them. Soon he fired, and in ten seconds again; then there was confused action, one bear falling down, the others rushing about with loud fierce cries, amid which the hunter's too could be distinguished; the mountain fairly echoed. I much feared he was lost, but soon, in his red shirt, he appeared on a rock; he had cried out, in Spanish for more balls. The bear was rolled down, and butchered before the wagons passed.[35]

It is clear that Colonel Cooke admired this courageous guide, who was now in his early forties and no longer young, but who had exceptional skills and abilities forged by twenty years of experience in the West. Cooke was grateful for Jean-Baptiste's many contributions to the success of the

---

[34]Cooke, "Journal," entry November 21, 1846; A. W. Hafen, "Jean-Baptiste Charbonneau," 89 n.26. [35]Cooke, "Journal," entry November 25, 1846: 131, 134.

expedition, much as William Clark had been grateful for the contributions of his parents on his historic expedition forty years before. Perhaps Jean-Baptiste was reunited with his adoptive brother at some point, since Captain Clark's eldest son, Meriwether Lewis Clark, just four years Jean-Baptiste's junior, had served as a major in the Mexican War in the Missouri battalion of artillery.

The expedition was nearing its end. A journal entry for January 20, 1847, in the San Felipe Valley, noted the return of Jean-Baptiste from San Diego to report on the meager supplies there and to recommend instead that they sojourn at Warner's Ranch. This proved to be a very popular decision. All could enjoy bathing in the hot springs there, soaking off the months of dust from the trail.

Alcalde of San Luis Rey (1847–1848)

The Mexican War had brought Jean-Baptiste to the Pacific Ocean. This may well have been the first time he had laid eyes upon it since he had seen it from his mother's back over forty years before. He had been in the forefront of linking the East and West all his life, and soon there would be no more wild frontiers. Ironically, by opening the West to settlement, he had helped close it to the way of life he loved. Faced with the end of the trail, he decided to linger a while and try out the settled life. The war had come to a successful conclusion, and now American administrators were needed for the newly acquired lands. Most likely, it was Cooke's acclaim of Jean-Baptiste's usefulness and ability to speak and write Spanish that had contributed to his "promotion" to his first desk job—magistrate of San Luis Rey Mission north of San Diego, in present-day Oceanside, California.

Mission San Luis Rey, by Henry Miller, 1856.
Courtesy The Bancroft Library.

This mission, established by Spanish Franciscans in 1798, had been the largest of all the California missions until secularized by the Mexican government in 1834. It had been sold to Governor Pío Pico twelve years later, and the following year, in July 1847, Governor Richard B. Mason had converted it into an Indian sub-agency. When the troops arrived there on August 9, it began its new function, quartering the troops and governing the Indians living there. Captain Jesse Hunter of the Mormon Battalion was appointed its sub-Indian agent, and, on November 24, Governor Mason named Hunter's good friend, Jean-Baptiste Charbonneau, as its *alcalde* (magistrate). They were charged with the "care and protection of Indian servants and ex-neophytes, as well as the keeping in check of gentile bands. Statistics and information on manners and customs were also called for."[36] The friendship between these two battalion veterans deepened the following April 26 as Hunter's wife, Lydia, lay dying in great pain, a week-old infant at her side. She was one of the few white women who had accompanied the soldiers, and she was much loved. In a scene reminiscent of Jean-Baptiste's own mother's death, "Lydia's death touched the heart of the soldiers. The guide, Charbonneau, was very kind and helpful to Captain Hunter during this sad time."[37]

But why did Jean-Baptiste take the job? It was not for the money—*alcaldes* served without pay. The "care and protection" and the "statistics and information" aspects may have appealed to his sense of public duty. Governor Clark had raised him to respect public service, education, and the need to protect the Indians. Indeed, one of Jean-Baptiste's first deeds was to establish an Indian school.[38] It was the "keeping in check" part that came to rankle. He had a different perspective on the "Indian problem" than his superiors, being half-Indian himself, and repressing the mission Indians did not sit well. Like Clark three decades earlier, he was perceived as too tolerant, and before long he was even accused of planning an insurrection. He denied the charges in writing in April 1848, but soon resigned anyway as a matter of conscience. Indians were being treated as slaves, caught in a system of endless obligation. In reference to the plight of one of the Indians, he complained of a system that would "sentence helpless Indians to slavery in order that they might pay for the liquor received in excess of the 12½ cents, their day's

---

[36] A. W. Hafen, "Jean-Baptiste Charbonneau," 90 n.27, citing H. H.Bancroft, *History of California* 1925, V: 568.
[37] Ricketts, *The Mormon Battalion*, 136.
[38] Hunsaker, *Sacagawea Speaks*, 90.

wages for labor." Adding these debts to other obligations, they would "never emerge from debt and slavery."[39]

On July 24, 1848, Colonel J. D. Stevenson, commander of the Southern Military District, sent a packet to Governor Mason which:

> Encloses the resignation of J.B. Charbonneau as Alcalde for San Luis Rey, and says that he has done his duty to the best of his ability but being "a half-breed Indian of the U.S. is regarded by the people as favoring the Indians more than he should do, and hence there is much complaint against him."[40]

That his good friend, sub-Indian agent Jesse Hunter, sympathized with Jean-Baptiste's stance is implied by his offer to resign as well. Instead, Hunter was granted a six-month leave that December, and the two men soon decided to head north for Sutter's Mill. As fate would have it, James Marshall had discovered gold there just a few months back. The Sacramento Valley was the place for an adventurous man to be that year, and that is where we find the next account of Jean-Baptiste Charbonneau. What exhilaration he must have felt to be liberated from the stifling life of a bureaucrat and to be riding along the northbound trails once more!

---

[39] Quoted in Anderson, "A Charbonneau Family Portrait," 18, from *Missouri and Missionaries* series of 1921 by Father Zephyrin Englehardt. McLeod ("Heritage: Jean-Baptiste Charbonneau, Cultured Mountain Man," 22) cites a record in the Santa Barbara Mission archives in which Jean-Baptiste sentenced the Indian Flujenjencia into the service of store owner, Don José Pico, until payment of a $51.37½ debt could be worked off out of wages of 12½ cents per day. Furtwangler takes Jean-Baptiste to task for participating in a system that exploited Indians and for occasionally imposing severe sentences, stating "as a guide, interpreter, prospector, and minor official, he had a hand in displacing or exploiting aboriginal peoples and ways of life . . . hard at work supporting white invaders" ("Sacagawea's Son as a Symbol," 311). This assessment fails to put Jean-Baptiste's life in the context of his times. Unlike most, he did speak out against this system and he did resign. If he is to be condemned for his part, then one must also condemn Jefferson, Lewis and Clark, and all the men of the era who had a hand in opening the West.

[40] A. W. Hafen ("Jean-Baptiste Charbonneau," 91 n.28) cites Bandini Documents and Unbound Documents, San Diego Archives, 328–33 (in the Bancroft Library, Univ. of Calif., Berkeley).

Chapter Seven

Gold Rush to Trail's End

Mr. Charbonneau was of pleasant manners, intelligent, well read in the topics of the day, and was generally esteemed in the community in which he lived, as a good meaning and inoffensive man.
—*Editor,* Placer Herald, *July 7, 1866, Auburn, California*[1]

Gold Fever

The sleepy settlement founded by John Sutter in 1839 exploded into excitement nine years later when James Marshall discovered gold at Coloma while building Sutter's lumber mill. By that May 1848, when Claude Chana found more gold in the Auburn Ravine, the stampede was well underway. For many, the call of California's gold rush was the voice of Greed, but, for men like Jean-Baptiste, it had more to do with adventure, freedom, and a man's life among other men in the out-of-doors than with finding gold. There is no indication he ever "struck it rich" or that he ever wanted to. The Indian in him rejected avarice, and his whole life illustrated that he was content with the simple life of a lone bachelor.[2]

---

[1] A. W. Hafen, "Jean-Baptiste Charbonneau," 94, quoting *The Placer Herald*, July 7, 1866, obituary. A copy of the original is on file at the Placer County Auburn Library.
[2] Parkman (*The Oregon Trail*, 228) discusses the willingness of western Indians to give away or destroy their possessions. Anthropologists have found that egali- *(continued, next page)*

He did, however, have good friends from the old days—men who, like him, had spent decades on the plains and in the mountains—and he was happy to meet up with them again and tell the old tales. And there were plenty of newcomers streaming in to hear them as well. By July 1849, the banks of the North and Middle Forks of the American River had seen an influx of 1,500 to 2,000 miners, with more arriving every day.[3]

One of the most noteworthy was Jim Beckwourth, whose life matched Jean-Baptiste's in its singularity. Beckwourth was a black Mountain Man of mixed slave and slave owner descent who had left Virginia behind for the life of a fur trader. He had spent many years among the Indians, was war chief of the Crows for a time, and his bravery was legendary.[4] Since around 1840, when both he and Jean-Baptiste were working for Bent and St. Vrain, their trails had crossed many times. In 1846, Beckwourth had opened a hotel in Santa Fe, and when the action moved to northern California for the gold rush, he figured he would try his luck there. He later wrote that, in the spring of 1849, he had found "Chapineau" on Murderer's Bar in the Middle Fork of the American River, a couple miles south of Auburn, and moved in with him until the rainy season in November.[5] Apparently, the two men then decided to become partners in the hotel business. An old school chum of Jean-Baptiste from St. Louis, James Haley White, who was in the West in 1850, later wrote that he had seen "Choboneau" on the road from Sacramento to Cold Springs and Placerville when he

---

tarian societies find ways to maintain the equal distribution of wealth, because their way of life can only be maintained if wealth does not accumulate in the hands of a few. These are values Jean-Baptiste would have learned as a boy and applied to the simple lifestyle he maintained all his life.
[3]Dorothy Sanborn (*Chronology of Auburn, California, 1848–1910*) summarizes *The Placer Herald*, July 1849.   [4]See, for example, Parkman, *The Oregon Trail*, 106.
[5]Elinor Wilson, *Jim Beckwourth: Black Mountain Man and War Chief of the Crows*, 122.

stopped at the inn kept by Beckwourth and Jean-Baptiste.[6] Of course, the partners tried their luck in the gold fields as well and, over the next few years, got out whenever they could to their claims on the Middle Fork of the American River and elsewhere.[7]

Both men were highly regarded by their fellow miners. *The Placer Herald* reported on June 24, 1849, that Kentucky miner "Tom Buckner's heart was gladdened by the appearance of other white men, not hostile, at his camp, in the person of J.B. Charbonneau, Jim Beckwourth, and Sam Mayers, all noted mountaineers."[8] It is ironic that Jean-Baptiste and Jim Beckwourth were described as "white men," but comradeship often affects perception. They were "one of us," therefore "white" in the eyes of men like Tom Buckner. This sort of camaraderie may go a long way towards explaining the call of the West to men like Jean-Baptiste and Jim Beckwourth. In the East they would have been marginalized and considered inferior, but in the West of the Mountain Men they were seen as equals and respected as individuals for their achievements. Unfortunately, as civilization encroached and more Easterners came West, their prejudices would come West with them.

Jean-Baptiste remained in the Auburn area for about

---

[6]Bonner (*The Life and Adventures of James P. Beckwourth*, 509 n.16) cites James Haley White, *St Louis and Its Men Fifty Years Ago*, 3.

[7]Charles G. Clark, *Men of the Lewis and Clark Expedition*, 149. A letter from Lincoln, California, archivist Gerald E. Logan, dated January 14, 1991 (on file at the Placer County Auburn Library), states that Murderer's Bar proved to be a wonderful place for gold, and that a J. D. Galbraith worked the "Big Crevice" at Murderer's Bar to the depth of twelve or fifteen feet in 1850. But whether or not Jean-Baptiste made much himself from this strike is not known.

[8]Myron Angel, ed., *History of Placer County, California*, 71; A. W. Hafen, "Jean-Baptiste Charbonneau," 92; Sanborn (*Chronology of Auburn, California*, June 24, 1849) notes that *The Placer Herald* reported on June 24, 1849, that Thomas M. Buckner had been joined by J. B. Charbonneau, Jim Beckwourth, and Sam Myers on the Middle Fork. According to James K. Woodworth and William G. Wilson ("Murderer's Bar: A Name from History," 8), Buckner was the first recorded white visitor to Murderer's Bar, arriving soon after gold was discovered.

eighteen years and watched it evolve. He was still a newcomer when California became the thirty-fourth state of the Union in 1850. Placer County was created that same year, and Auburn was named its seat the next. From the beginning, he witnessed many compelling events as, all around him, thousands of men worked at a frenzied pace to find that magical scoop of earth that would make their dreams come true. An example is this colorful scene, which was reported by a correspondent for *The Placer Herald* in May 1850:

> The noise and confusion in the blacksmith shop where I am trying to write this is deafening. Miners are coming and going with their gold-digging tools for resharpening, and the braying of donkeys is disturbing. Near the door, three Chinamen are scooping up dirt to wash at the creek.[9]

Murderer's Bar

This was the "Wild West" to be sure. Federal law allowed free access to land for prospecting, but holding on to it was another matter. A claim lasted only as long as a shotgun could defend it. A good example of the violence of the times is provided by the very scene of Jean-Baptiste's inn, Murderer's Bar. Legend has it that in 1849, Tom Buckner, with his partner, Ezekial Merritt, and an Indian boy called Peg, were the first miners to come to this bar, which was the largest sand and gravel bar on the Middle Fork of the American River. On arriving, they saw no white men, but they did see signs of a great struggle, evidenced by tufts of hair from both a white man and an Indian. No bodies were found, but calcined bone fragments unearthed nearby suggested to them that Indians may have cremated and buried both protagonists. The next day Buckner carved the words "MURDERER'S BAR" into the bark of a white elder growing beside the river.

---

[9]Sanborn, *Chronology of Auburn, California*, summary of *The Placer Herald* for May 1850.

The name stuck and, almost overnight, this flat spot along the river, previously used by only a few of the indigenous Nisenan of the Maidu Tribe, burst into a full-blown town made of wood and canvas. This new boomtown boasted not only the inn run by Jean-Baptiste and Beckwourth, but one other inn as well, along with a blacksmith shop, butcher shop, plaza, fourteen saloons, two general merchandise stores, and the Round Tent saloon and gambling hall. The miners on the bar kept their ears pricked for a horn's blast from the hilltop, signaling the arrival of the mule train with new supplies of liquor. Someone would then fire a rifle to alert all the miners up and down the river to descend on the Round Tent, where a good time would be had by all until the liquor ran out.[10] This scene must have reminded Jean-Baptiste of the old rendezvous, where the reward for many hard days of work was the arrival of the supplies from St. Louis and plenty of liquor for all hands.

Murderer's Bar continued to live up to its name in July 1850, when Jean-Baptiste may have witnessed the duel that was fought there. Although shots were fired, both missed their marks. A shootout the following month, however, proved less lucky for a man named Beck. He was killed by a fellow miner with the ominous name of Black Walker.

As if 1850 were not eventful enough at Murderer's Bar, Nature weighed in with her own violence in the form of two disastrous floods. The first came in January when the river rose sixty feet, washing away all the miners' belongings and leaving them without shelter or food. This was followed by a flash flood in September.[11] This second disaster was the

---

[10] Woodworth and Wilson, "Murderer's Bar: A Name from History," 10.

[11] Sanborn, *Chronology of Auburn, California*, summary of *The Placer Herald* for January 9, July, August, and September 1850. Although Woodworth and Wilson ("Murderer's Bar A Name from History," 10) put the September flood in 1849, *The Placer Herald* reported it for September 1850.

Bar on the Middle Fork of the American River near Auburn, California. *Photo by Susan Colby.*

more cruel. The men had just completed the backbreaking job of constructing a mile-long flume to divert the river so that they could mine the riverbed. All of the wood for the flume had been painstakingly hauled in and assembled over the long, hot summer. Finally, the job was done. It was Saturday night and the men celebrated. On Sunday, two miners tested the newly exposed riverbed and retrieved an incredible nine pounds of gold. The omens looked good for huge rewards on Monday. During the night, however, ominous clouds accumulated in the mountains and soon great torrents swept down the ravines, inundating the flume and sweeping it away along with the miners' hopes.[12]

Auld Lang Syne

A curious turn of events that August nearly reunited Jean-Baptiste with his old mentor, Duke Paul of Württemberg. Like so many others from all parts of the globe, Duke Paul had been drawn to the phenomenon of the gold rush, and he kept a record of his trip. Lost for many years, this journal mysteriously reappeared in 1929.[13]

After his return to Germany from America in 1831, Duke Paul had won much acclaim for the quality of his collections in Mergentheim and for his contributions to research in the natural sciences. He had "amassed the largest-ever natural science collection" (consisting of over 100,000 specimens) and had become as well-regarded as the famous naturalist Baron von Humboldt.[14] In addition, the University of Tübingen had awarded him doctoral degrees in philosophy and medicine. Unfortunately, none of this acclaim was accompanied by funding. Times were bad for the aristocracy and the duke's finances had been dwindling over the years. Following the social unrest of 1848, his financial situation turned disastrous. According to Von Sachsen-Altenburg, Duke Paul eventually had to go into hiding, and his next trip abroad was more of an escape than an expedition.

Now he was returning to the New World after an absence of nearly twenty years, anxious to see how the West had pro-

---

[12]Woodworth and Wilson, "Murderer's Bar: A Name from History," 10.
[13]See John A. Hussey, ed., *Early Sacramento: Glimpses*, 7; Von Sachsen-Altenburg and Dyer, *Duke Paul of Wuerttemberg*, 97–98; Furtwangler, "Sacagawea's Son as a Symbol," 306–7. Unfortunately, the translations of both early translators of the journals, Louis C. Butscher and Friedrich Bauser, have been found to be questionable. See, for example, note 16, below.   [14]Von Sachsen-Altenburg and Dyer, *Duke Paul of Wuerttemberg*, 26.

gressed. In the spring of 1849, after visiting his favorite American city, New Orleans, he continued westward to Texas and Mexico for scientific observations. Several months later, he sailed from Mazatlan to San Pedro and on to San Francisco. Since one object of his journey was to see the gold rush for himself, he proceeded on to the Sacramento Valley, where he joined John Sutter in the Fourth of July parade, and from there he pressed on to the gold fields. Although acquainted with the hard life led in the West, he found the life of a miner particularly miserable. Contrary to romantic legend, little profit was realized by most as they led lives replete with hazard and privation. He commiserated with them as they worked all day in the sun while standing in icy river waters that yielded barely enough gold to cover their expenses.[15]

Back with John Sutter on the Hock farm in Marysville, Duke Paul admired the fine-looking Indians employed there. He noted that Mr. Sutter treated them well and thus had no shortage of Indians willing to work for him. While watching these Indians in native costume chasing their wild horses over the wheat to thresh it, Duke Paul reflected that some of them were Shoshoni, and that "One of these Snake Indians was a very bright fellow and reminded me of the B Charboneau who followed me to Europe in 1823 and whose mother was a Scho-sho-né."[16]

---

[15]Lincoln, California, archivist Gerald E. Logan estimates that most miners were lucky to make two or three dollars a day in 1850, when gold was worth about seventeen dollars an ounce. His letter, dated January 14, 1991, is on file at the Placer County Auburn Library.

[16]Furtwangler ("Sacagawea's Son as a Symbol," 307) offers this translation by Charles Upson Clark as superior to that of Butscher, which was quoted by Hussey, ed., *Early Sacramento: Glimpses*, 59. The following is Butscher's elaborated translation, which has been widely quoted: "Among these latter [Shoshones] was a handsome youth who reminded me, on account of his startling likeness, of a lad of the same tribe whom I took to Europe with me from a fur-trading post at the mouth of the Kansas, in western Mississippi in the fall of 1823, and who was my companion there on all my travels over Eu-

Clearly Duke Paul was remembering his protégé with affection. Little did he know that just a few miles away, that same lad, now a man of forty-five, labored in the waters of the American River. How interesting an account of that reunion would have been! But alas, there is no indication in his journals that Duke Paul was aware of this fact or that the two men ever did see each other again.

Duke Paul's journal also gives us a glimpse of the cruel prejudices confronting Indians at that time. He could well understand why there had been violent uprisings. He witnessed the "vile element of Anglo-Saxon Americans who have been committing theft, arson, violence against their women and murder among the tribe." He took heart when John Sutter assured him that "the respectable, law-abiding settlers had decided to resort to the most drastic measures in order to protect these red men against the brutality of these vagabond rowdies and jailbirds."[17]

Indeed, race relations were poor all over the West by then. Harriet Munnick, for example, wrote of the sorry treatment of the *métis* in the Oregon Territory at that time: "The metis thus had two strikes against him: the dislike of the pioneer

---

rope and northern Africa until 1829, when he returned with me to America in 1829. This latter was the son of a Shoshone woman who with her husband, a Canadian Frenchman, accompanied the Messrs. Lewis and Clarke on their expedition to the Pacific Coast in 1804–1806, the one as guide and the other as interpreter. The boy was born on the return trip, and when still quite young, General William Clark asked the mother's permission to take him to St. Louis in order that he might have him educated at the Catholic Brothers' Seminary." (Since there was no "Catholic Brothers' Seminary" when Jean-Baptiste first came to St. Louis, Butscher's tendency to elaborate and fabricate is evident.) There is yet a third translation offered by Bauser as "One of these Snakes was a fine young lad, quite intelligent, who reminded me strangely and with a certain sadness of B. Charbonneau, who had followed me in 1823 to Europe, and whose mother was of the tribe of the Sho-sho-ne" See Furtwangler ("Sacagawea's Son as a Symbol," n.31) as to Charles Upson Clark, trans., "Extracts from the Journals of Prince Paul of Württemberg, Year 1850," *Southwestern Journal of Anthropology* 15 (1959): 252; quoted in John A. Hussey, ed., *Early Sacramento: Glimpses*, 59–60.

[17] Hussey, ed., *Early Sacramento: Glimpses*, 65.

American for his French father and the discrimination against himself for his mixed ancestry."[18]

No doubt Jean-Baptiste suffered insults from time to time from some of this element, but he did not stand alone, since his brother Mountain Men stood with him. Given Jean-Baptiste's history of defending Indian rights, it is most likely that he was among those respectable, law-abiding settlers, referred to above, who defended the Indians against the ignorant rabble.

Duke Paul was in no hurry to return to the problems he had left behind in Europe. He went south again to Panama, on to New Orleans, and then to points north. Returning to St. Louis, he boarded the steamboat *Pocahontas* on August 31, 1851, and headed for the Kaw River near present-day Kansas City, the place where he had first met Jean-Baptiste twenty-eight years before. From there he proceeded overland to Fort Laramie. Heading back east along the Platte River in October, he nearly perished in a blizzard, arriving in St. Louis much the worse for wear on the last day of the year—no doubt very much aware of all of his fifty-four years. The time had come to leave his western travels behind forever for the realities that awaited him in his homeland.

Returning to Familiar Scenes

Meanwhile, Jean Baptiste was aging, too. Before long, the gold played out, the claims were abandoned, and the miners either returned home or settled in California. As far as we know, Jean-Baptiste had no family to return to. He had gone as far west as he could go, and he decided to stay on in the Auburn area. In 1852, records show that "John Charbonneau's" work as "Assistant Surveyor" earned him

---

[18]Harriet D. Munnick, "Jean-Baptiste Lucier, *dit* Gardipe," 209.

forty-eight dollars.[19] As he approached the half-century mark, he probably could not have withstood the rigors of a mountain man's life again. If he is, however, the "Sharaneau" mentioned in an old history book of Placer County, he did retain some of the vigor he was known for back in 1844, when he was described as the "best man on foot on the plains or in the Rocky Mountains."[20] This book tells of Manhattan Bar on the Middle Fork of the American River and "a Cherokee Indian, by name Sharaneau, who lived there before the telegraph times [and] was used as a rapid dispatch bearer and runner."[21]

Most likely, Jean-Baptiste supported himself in various humble ways like this over the years, earning just enough to support his simple lifestyle. In any case, it was in this general area that the census found him in 1860 at the age of fifty-five, when his address was "P.O. Secret Ravine," a few miles out of Auburn.[22] By 1861, after the telegraph had rendered runners obsolete, the Placer County Directory lists him as "John B. Charbonneau," a clerk at the Orleans Hotel in Auburn. He was again supporting himself in the hotel business, as he had with Beckwourth a few years back, and he was leading a modest life in harmony with his fellow citizens.

But the embers of his old passion were extinguished neither by old age nor by city life, and the great population

---

[19]List of bills and accounts paid in cash, Section 5, Schedule B, 1852 Treasurer's Report in Angel, *History of Placer County California*, 143.

[20]*William Boggs Journal, 1844–45*, quoted in H. P. Howard, *Sacajawea*, 173.

[21]W. B. Lardner and M. J. Brock, *History of Placer and Nevada Counties, California*, 178; also see letter on file at the Placer County Auburn Library, dated January 14, 1991, from archivist Gerald E. Logan to D. Beverly Hughes. Mr. Logan believed this "Sharaneau to be Charbonneau" since Manhattan Bar is only about six or seven miles downstream from Murderer's Bar, and it is likely Jean-Baptiste worked at several mining camps. Coe (*The Telegraph: A History*, 38) states that the telegraph arrived in Sacramento and Carson City by 1860.

[22]A. W. Hafen, "Jean-Baptiste Charbonneau," 93; he is listed in the census as a miner, age fifty-seven, born in Missouri.

explosion in California only fueled this yearning for the wilderness. While the population of the entire state had been just 14,000 in 1848, by the end of 1849, it had ballooned to over 100,000. Jean-Baptiste had not seen such crowds since leaving Europe. And it seemed there would be no letup even after the gold rush ended, as civilized folks arrived to replace the rugged miners. By the summer of 1864, as the Central Pacific Railroad approached Auburn with its promise to join West to East, the handwriting was on the wall.[23] Soon he could no longer resist the call of the north wind, and he found just the opportunity he craved. As a friend put it, "The reported discoveries of gold in Montana, and the rapid peopling of the Territory, excited the imagination of the old trapper, and he determined to return to the scenes of his youth."[24] Some time in the spring of 1866, now aged sixty-one, Jean-Baptiste set out with two companions on his final adventure.[25] This poignant tribute on the editorial page of the July 7, 1866, *Placer Herald* summarizes what followed:

---

[23]Derek Avery, *The Complete History of North American Railways*, 36. In June 1854, the Central Pacific issued its first timetable for the thirty-one miles from Sacramento to Newcastle (just outside Auburn), bringing passengers and goods thrice daily. The East and West lines were linked in 1869.

[24]A. W. Hafen, "Jean-Baptiste Charbonneau," 94, quoting the obituary on the editorial page of *The Placer Herald*, Auburn, California, dated July 7, 1866. A copy is on file at the Placer County Auburn Library.

[25]Notice of his death, in a note dated May 16, 1866, is mentioned in *The Owyhee Avalanche* newspaper, June 2, 1866; A. W. Hafen, "Jean-Baptiste Charbonneau," 94; *Placer Herald* obituary copy on file at Placer County Auburn Library. An alternative version of Jean-Baptiste's death was offered by Hebard (*Sacajawea*, 147) in which she stated that Jean-Baptiste and his brother, Bazil, spent many years among their mother's people in Wind River, and that Jean-Baptiste died there in 1885 at the age of eighty, seemingly having forgotten how to read and write. That version, along with Hebard's claim that Sacagawea died on the Wind River reservation in central Wyoming at the age of one hundred, have been widely discredited. Anderson ("A Charbonneau Family Portrait," 4) summarizes the factual evidence against Hebard's version. Also see *Michigan's Habitant Heritage, Journal of the French-Canadian Heritage Society of Michigan* 25, no 2 (April 2004): 104, in which a genealogical researcher tentatively lists a Louis and Susan Charbonneau-Provencale-Leblanc as parents of two brothers: a John B. Charbonneau, born about 1818, and a Bazil Charbonneau, born about 1823. Perhaps this is the family that Hebard met. More research is needed.

J. B. Charbonneau

Death of a California Pioneer—We are informed by Mr. Dana Perkins,[26] that he has received a letter announcing the death of J. B. Charbonneau, who left this country some weeks ago, with two companions, for Montana Territory. The letter is from one of the party, who says Mr. C., [*sic*] was taken sick with mountain fever, on the Owyhee, and died after a short illness.

Mr. Charbonneau was known to most of the pioneer citizens of this region of country, being himself one of the first adventurers (into territory now known as Placer county) upon the discovery of gold; where he has remained with little intermission until his recent departure for the new gold field, Montana, which, strangely enough, was the land of his birth, whither he was returning in the evening of life, to spend the few remaining days that he felt was in store for him.

Mr. Charbonneau was born in the western wilds, and grew up a hunter, trapper, and pioneer, among that class of men of which Bridger, Beckwourth, and the other noted trappers of the woods were the representatives. He was born in the country of the Crow Indians—his father being a Canadian Frenchman, and his mother a half breed of the Crow tribe. He had, however, better opportunities than most of the rough spirits, who followed the calling of trapper, as when a young man he went to Europe and spent several years, where he learned to speak, as well as write several languages. At the breaking out of the Mexican War he was on the frontiers, and upon the organization of the Mormon Battalion he was engaged as a guide and came with them to California.

Subsequently upon the discovery of gold, he, in company with Jim Beckwourth, came upon the North Fork of the American river, and for a time it is said were mining partners.

Our acquaintance with Charbonneau dates back to '52, when we found him a resident of this county, where he has continued to reside almost continuously since—having given up frontier life. The reported discoveries of gold in Montana, and the rapid peopling of the Territory, excited the imagination of the old trapper, and he determined to return to the scenes of his youth.—Though strong of purpose, the weight of years was too much for the hardships of the trip undertaken, and he now sleeps alone by the bright waters of the Owyhee.

---

[26]McLeod ("Heritage: Jean-Baptiste Charbonneau, Cultured Mountain Man," 23) reports that Dana Perkins was listed in the 1860 census as a local hotelkeeper.

Our information is very meager of the history of the deceased—a fact we much regret, as he was of a class that for years lived among stirring and eventful scenes.

The old man, on departing for Montana, gave us a call, and said he was going to leave California, probably for good, as he was about returning to familiar scenes. We felt then as if we met him for the last time.

Mr. Charbonneau was of pleasant manners, intelligent, well read in the topics of the day, and was generally esteemed in the community in which he lived, as a good meaning and inoffensive man.

Final Character Clues

This *Placer Herald* tribute contains several clues to the personality of Jean-Baptiste Charbonneau. Before leaving town, the old man had called on his friend, the paper's editor, to say farewell. He seems to have been fully aware that, at his age, he would never make it back from such a venture, but it did not matter. It is doubtful reaching the Montana gold fields mattered much either. He was going back to the mountains—"to familiar scenes." He would see the Rockies again, rendezvous in Montana, spin a few yarns, and take one last grasp at the life he loved.

What else can we read between the lines? Jean-Baptiste was not a boaster. The editor, a friend who had known him for fourteen years, knew nothing of his association with the Lewis and Clark expedition or his adoption by William Clark. Yet he did know about the days as a student in Europe, as a hunter and trapper, as an associate of Beckwourth and Bridger, and as a guide for the Mormon Battalion. In his final years, Jean-Baptiste took credit only for what he had achieved by his own efforts. The description of his mother as half-Crow suggests that Jean-Baptiste never discussed his mother. Even his good friend, Beckwourth, thought Jean-Baptiste's mother was a Crow,[27] while Boggs believed her to have been a Blackfoot.[28] Actually, Sacagawea was proud to have been born a Shoshoni, whose traditional enemies were the Blackfoot and the Crow. Recall that Jean-Baptiste also did not discuss his mother on the 1843 expedition with Clark's kin. Perhaps he deliberately protected the memory of his mother by not discussing her with anyone.

Some suggest that Jean-Baptiste tried to "play down or suppress his Indian parentage."[29] This theory is untenable. Nearly all contemporaries who wrote of Jean-Baptiste recognized him as a "half-breed" with a mother from a western tribe. The only support offered for this theory is the quote from the forty-niner (cited on page 165 herein) calling Jean-Baptiste a white man. But the speaker called Jim Beckwourth white as well, although he was widely known as a mulatto. Was Jim Beckwourth too trying to pass for white? I think not.

The *Placer Herald* editor regretted that he had never drawn out Jean-Baptiste, so he had never heard the full story. Pleasant and "inoffensive," Jean-Baptiste had sought no attention or acclaim. In a place where settlers were quick to exclude "half-breeds," he was "esteemed"—not because he was the adopted son of William Clark, nor because he had been the protégé of a duke of Europe, but because of his own achievements and demeanor. The argument by the critic continues—if the "inflated notion" of Jean-Baptiste's European experience is indeed true, then "at least two authors [Grace Hebard and Ann Hafen] are embarrassed by Charbonneau's subsequent life story." He reasons, "how could such a man of refinement spend the rest of his life at

---
[27]Bonner, *The Life and Times of James P. Beckwourth*, 528
[28]*William Boggs Journal, 1844–1845*, quoted in H. P. Howard, *Sacajawea*, 173.
[29]Furtwangler, "Sacagawea's Son as a Symbol," 312.

hard labor on western trails, far from books and the pleasures of the fine intellect?"[30] As a matter of fact, he was not that "far from books and the pleasures of the fine intellect," since the classics were available and prized in the Old West. For example, when Francis Parkman was at Fort Laramie in 1846, he was offered the works of Shakespeare, Byron, and the Old Testament. Perhaps this critic misses the point. There are many ways to satisfy a "fine intellect." Here was a successful life—a melding of his father's trail-blazing pioneer heritage, his mother's resourceful Indian heritage, and the heritage of knowledge and "good meaning" that he obtained from his Jeffersonian mentors.

This critic does make a valid point, however, in cautioning against viewing Jean-Baptiste as a symbol. One could argue that it was William Clark who first envisioned his symbolic role. As an educated Indian, he symbolized all of Clark's hopes for the future of the West. In our era, he can, like his mother, easily capture the romantic imagination and be cast as a flawless hero when, of course, he was a man of

---

[30]Ibid., 308–9. Hebard's account of Jean-Baptiste's adult years has been discredited. If it were true, Furtwangler would have a point. As it is not true, it is pointless to bring up her potential "embarrassment" here. Although Furtwangler ("Sacagawea's Son as a Symbol," 310–11) rejects Hafen's "romantic" idea that Jean-Baptiste "chose wilderness" in a positive way, he offers instead a psychological alternative involving "a vain chase west, pursuing the phantom of the exploring father-patron-commander who had vanished—until he himself became a knowledgeable guide and man of the western trail." But has this alternative notion any basis in fact? If there is any reason to conclude that Jean-Baptiste's life was a "vain chase west," I have failed to find it. (In note 41, Furtwangler acknowledges that Jean-Baptiste's contemporaries also deduced that his western life was his choice, but Furtwangler seems to believe that he knows better.) Unfortunately, we many never get close enough to the real Jean-Baptiste Charbonneau to understand his motivations, but the reality is that he did indeed "choose wilderness" from among many other options for as long as he was physically able to do so. Had he chosen to remain in St. Louis, undoubtedly Clark would have accommodated him with a government job, or his godfather would have found him a job in the business world. Likewise, there is no reason to believe he could not have returned to Europe with Duke Paul had he chosen to do so, since the duke kept another foreign boy with him there until the lad's death ten years later.

flesh and blood. As the forty-niner saw "white" men when he encountered Jean-Baptiste and Jim Beckwourth, so too do we all tend to see who and what inspires us when we follow Clark's "little dancing boy" through to the end of his incredible life's journey. Because there are so many gaps in the historical record, it is easy to fill them in to meet our own needs and expectations. Be that as it may, reviewing the broad outline of his life from its auspicious beginnings with the Corps of Discovery to his education in St. Louis and Europe, and on to the Rocky Mountain rendezvous and the Santa Fe and Mormon Battalion trails, to old San Diego and Sacramento, how can one keep from saying, here was a life of freedom and adventure, the likes of which will never be possible again?

And it all came to a fitting ending as well. Jean-Baptiste did not make it to the Rockies, but he had crossed the Sierras and would have seen the beautiful Owyhee Mountains of southeastern Oregon before him. He recognized them, of course, from the 1830s when he used to approach them from the opposite direction. As they neared the Owyhee River, did his mind drift back to the summer of 1832 when he and Bridger had taken their leave of Nathaniel Wyeth at its confluence with the Snake? Old friends and old tales may have filled his thoughts as their horses ambled eastward. But he was no longer young and resilient and the cold was sometimes bitter. The snows had been melting in the mountains and frigid waters had swollen the river. Crossing the ford just below the junction of Jordan Creek and the Owyhee River, freezing waters soaked his clothes and the cold April wind and rain held the dampness to him. Soon prostrate with fever, his friends transported him twenty-five miles northeast of the river to the nearest way station, the fortified

Interpretive sign at gravesite of Jean-Baptiste Charbonneau.

Rededication of refurbished gravesite at Donner, Oregon, in March 1999 (a project of the Oregon chapter of the National Lewis and Clark Trail Heritage Foundation). *Both photos courtesy of Keith Hay.*

shelter at Inskip's station. He drew his last breath there, about 250 miles from his mother's birthplace.[31] Some call his final illness "pneumonia," and some "mountain fever." Metaphorically speaking, he had a case of the latter all his life and was content to die of it.

Jean-Baptiste passed away on or just before May 16, 1866, and was laid to rest near Inskip's Station at the mouth of Cow Creek in the present-day eastern Oregon town of Danner. On March 14, 1973, his gravesite was designated a Registered National Historic Place and his remarkable life was commemorated by this plaque:

> OREGON HISTORY
> Jean-Baptiste Charbonneau
> 1805–1866
>
> This site marks the final resting place of the youngest member of the Lewis and Clark expedition. Born to Sacajawea and Toussaint Charbonneau at Fort Mandan (North Dakota) on February 11, 1805. Baptiste and his mother symbolized the peaceful nature of the "Corps of Discovery." Educated by Captain William Clark at St. Louis, Baptiste at age 18, [sic] traveled to Europe where he spent six years, becoming fluent in English, German, French and Spanish. Returning to America in 1829, he ranged the Far West for nearly four decades, as mountain man, guide, interpreter, magistrate and forty niner. In 1866, he left the California gold fields for a new strike in Montana, contracted pneumonia enroute, reached "Inskip's Ranche", here, and died on May 16, 1866.

The site was rededicated June 24, 2000, and has been visited by many relatives and admirers over the years, including his distant cousins, Vincent Charbonneau and son David, who made the pilgrimage from New York shortly before Vincent's eighty-seventh birthday. Although Jean-Baptiste left no verified descendents, the Charbonneau family goes proudly forward.

---

[31] Anderson, "Sacajawea's Papoose"; Nelson, *Interpreters with Lewis and Clark*, 122.

Jean-Baptiste was not the last of the Corps of Discovery to pass away. Sergeant Patrick Gass holds that distinction, having lived until 1870, just short of ninety-nine years. Jean-Baptiste did, however, have the distinction of being the most widely traveled of the expedition veterans. Even William Clark did not travel so far east as Germany or so far southwest as southern California.

In the end, Jean-Baptiste had kept faith with his parents and his guardian. He had fulfilled unspoken promises made in those early, hopeful days by remaining true to his tripartite heritage as an Indian, a French-Canadian fur trapper, and a Jeffersonian enlightened man. He had reconciled all three into an intelligent, admirable man in harmony with his fellow citizens, respectful of the public good, and inspired by an undying passion for the West. In his later years, he had become the "citizen Indian" envisioned by Clark, mindful of his heritage while living peacefully among men of all cultures. If all those going west had followed his lead, how much more just and admirable western expansion would have been. Just below the surface of Clark's civilized Jeffersonian man, however, endured the French and Indian man of the wilderness. And it was this man who chose his closing scene.

In 1800, a young girl was pulled up onto a horse and spirited away from the mountains she loved. What joy she felt upon returning five years later—a joy experienced again in the spring of 1866 by her French-Indian son, Jean-Baptiste Charbonneau—

> I'm proud of de sam' blood in my vein
> I'm a son of de Nort' Win wance again. . . .[32]

---

[32] From the poem "The Voyageur" by William Henry Drummond, M.D.

Appendix

The Paternal Line of Jean-Baptiste Charbonneau

Marriages

I.

Olivier Charbonneau   20 December 1653   Marie Marguerite Garnier
                       Marans, France[1]   (Charles/Jeanne Labraye
                                             de Bagouges)

II.

Michel Charbonneau I   12 November 1692   Marguerite Denoyon
(Olivier/M. Marguerite Boucherville, Québec[2] (Jean/Marie Chauvin)
Garnier)

III.

Michel Charbonneau II   12 October 1722   Geneviève Richaume
(Michel/Marguerite   Boucherville, Québec[3] Babin Lacroix
Denoyon)   (Pierre Babin/
                                             Madeleine Richaume)

IV.

Jean-Baptiste Charbonneau I   1 March 1756   Marguerite Deniau
(Michel/Geneviève   Boucherville, Québec[4]   (Pierre/Angélique
Richaume Babin Lacroix)   Reguindeau)

V.

Toussaint Charbonneau   8 February 1805 (?)   Sacagawea
(Jean-Baptiste/Marguerite undocumented, ND[5]
Deniau)

VI.

Jean-Baptiste Charbonneau II
(Toussaint/Sacagawea)

---

[1]The marriage record for Olivier Charbonneau and Marie Marguerite Garnier was believed for years to have been lost in La Rochelle, France, to the fires of the Wars of Religion. Recently, however, it was located and was presented by the mayor to the visiting members of the Charbonneau Family Association of Québec. Their arrival in New France from La Rochelle is documented in *Programme de recherche en démographie historique* (cited as *PRDH* hereafter) #402987 and #403039.

[2]*Dictionnaire des Mariages Charbonneau* (cited as *DMC* hereafter) #2494, p. 180. *PRDH* #3843.   [3]*DMC* #2481, p. 179. *PRDH* #4008.

[4]*DMC* #1590, p. 115. *PRDH* #312793.

[5]There is no record of a legal marriage. This date is often given but is unverified. *DMC* #3087, p. 223.

Baptism, Birth, and Death Records

OLIVIER CHARBONNEAU: d. 28 Nov. 1687, Rivières des Prairies, Québec & Marie Marguerite Garnier b. 20 Dec. 1625, Marans, France; d., 2 Dec. 1701, Lachenaie, Québec[6]

MICHEL CHARBONNEAU I: bap. 2 Oct. 1666, Boucherville, Québec and d., 1 May 1724, Boucherville, Québec & Marguerite Denoyon b. 20 Aug. 1673, Boucherville, Québec; d. Mascouche, Quebec in 1745[7]

MICHEL CHARBONNEAU II: b. 22 Nov. 1699, Boucherville, Québec; d. 10 Dec. 1773, Boucherville, Québec & Geneviève Richaume Babin Lacroix b. 28 Dec. 1703, Boucherville, Québec; d. 26 Nov. 1741,Contrecoeur, Québec[8]

JEAN-BAPTISTE CHARBONNEAU I: b. 28 Aug. 1735, Boucherville, Québec; d. 17 June 1791, Détroit (Michigan) & Marguerite Deniau b. 19 April 1735, Longueuil, Québec, and she died there 16 Feb. 1797[9]

TOUSSAINT CHARBONNEAU: bap. 21 March 1767 (born 20 March 1767), Boucherville, Québec; death date unknown (1843?) & Sacagawea, date of birth unknown; d. 20 Dec. 1812 at Fort Manuel (SD)[10]

JEAN-BAPTISTE CHARBONNEAU II: bap. 28 Dec. 1809, St. Louis, MO (born 11 Feb. 1805, Fort Mandan, ND); d. 16 May 1866, Danner, Oregon[11]

---

[6] No birth record was ever found for Olivier Charbonneau, but he is thought to have been born in Marans, France, around 1611. His death and that of Marie Marguerite Garnier were verified in *DMC* by the Charbonneau Family Association in Quebec.

[7] *PRDH* #39858 (baptismal date of Michel Charbonneau, son of Olivier). Dates verified in *DMC* by the Charbonneau Family Association in Quebec, who also verified that Michel worked for the North West Fur Company for thirty-five years and that the brothers, Michel and Joseph, went to Detroit in 1707 for this company.

[8] Verified in *DMC* by the Charbonneau Family Association of Quebec.

[9] Ibid. A reproduction of the death record of Jean-Baptiste Charbonneau from Ste.-Anne-du-Détroit is in the possession of the author.

[10] *PRDH* #636682 verifies birth and baptism of Toussaint Charbonneau and his parentage. The *DMC* and the Charbonneau Family Association of Quebec concur with this birth-date and parentage for Toussaint Charbonneau.

[11] Jean-Baptiste Charbonneau's birth was witnessed and recorded by Meriwether Lewis in his journal and also in the journals of Orway, Gass, and Whitehouse. See documentation of his baptism in Bob Moore, "Pompey's Baptism, A recently discovered document sheds light on the christening of Jean Baptiste Charbonneau," 11. His death date was reported in the obituaries cited in Chapter 7. No marriages or offspring (other than the infant who died in Germany) have been documented for Jean-Baptiste (see Chapter 4, 111–12, and Chapter 6, 149–50n.17).

BIBLIOGRAPHY

Abel, Annie Holoise, ed. *F. A. Chardon, Chardon's Journal at Fort Clark, 1834–1839.* Lincoln: University of Nebraska Press, 1932.

Abert, James W. "The Journal of James W. Abert, from Bent's Fort to St. Louis in 1845." H. Bailey Carroll, ed. *Panhandle Plains Historical Review* 14, no. 2 (1941): 113.

Aikens, C. Melvin. *Archaeology of Oregon.* U.S. Department of the Interior, Bureau of Land Management, Oregon State Office, second edition, 1986.

Ambrose, Stephen E. *Undaunted Courage: Meriwether Lewis, Thomas Jefferson, and the Opening of the American West.* New York: Simon & Schuster, 1997.

American State Papers, 1820. Missouri Historical Society, St. Louis, Mo.

Anderson, Irving W. "J. B. Charbonneau, Son of Sacajawea." *Oregon Historical Quarterly* 71, no. 3 (September 1970): 247–264.

———. "Sacajawea's Papoose." Manuscript on file at the Auburn Placer County Library, based on "J. B. Charbonneau, Son of Sacajawea."

———. "Probing the Riddle of the Bird Woman." *Montana The Magazine of Western History* 23 (Autumn 1973).

———. "A Charbonneau Family Portrait: Biographical Sketches of Sacagawea, Jean Baptiste, and Toussaint Charbonneau." Brochure for the Fort Clatsop Historical Association, revised ed. 1992. Originally published in *America West Magazine* (March/April 1980).

Anderson, Irving W., and Blanche Schroer. "Sacagawea: Her Name and Destiny." *We Proceeded On* 25, no. 4 (November 1999): 6–10.

Angel, Myron, ed. *History of Placer County, California*. Oakland: Thompson & West, 1882.

Archibald, Robert. "Remembering Sheheke: Mandan Chief and American Patriot." *We Proceeded On* (February 2004): 10.

Avery, Derek, ed. *The Complete History of North American Railways*. London: Brian Trodd, 1989.

Bakeless, John. *Lewis and Clark: Partners in Discovery*. New York: William Morrow, 1947.

Bauser, Friedrich. "Biographical Facts Regarding Duke Paul of Wuerttemberg." *South Dakota Historical Collections* 19 (1938): 467.

Bek, William G., trans. "First Journal to America in the Years 1822–1824." *South Dakota Historical Collections* (1938): 4–474.

Boggs, William M. "The William M. Boggs Manuscript about Bent's Fort, Kit Carson, the Far West and Life among the Indians." In L.R. Hafen, ed., *Colorado Magazine* 7 (1930): 66–67.

Bonner, Thomas D. *The Life and Adventures of James P. Beckwourth as told to Thomas D. Bonner*. Lincoln: University of Nebraska Press, 1972.

Bowers, Alfred W. *Hidatsa Social and Ceremonial Organization*. Smithsonian Institution, Bureau of American Ethnology Bulletin no. 194, 1965.

Brackenridge, Henry M. "Journal of a Voyage up the Missouri River in 1811." In R.G. Thwaites, ed., *Early Western Travels* VI. Cleveland: Arthur H. Clark Company, 1904.

———. *Views of Louisiana*. Readex Microprint Corp., 1966.

Burt, Olive. *Sacajawea*. New York: Franklin Watts, 1978.

Carter, Harvey L. "Andrew Drips." In L. R. Hafen, ed. *Mountain Men and Fur Traders of the Far West*. Lincoln: University of Nebraska Press (1982): 332–345.

———. "Introduction." In L. R. Hafen, ed., *Mountain Fen and Fur Traders of the Far West*. Lincoln: University of Nebraska Press, 1982.

———. "Kit Carson." In L. R. Hafen, ed. *Mountain Men and Fur Traders of the Far West*. Lincoln: University of Nebraska Press (1982): 166–192.

Chalfant, William Y. *Dangerous Passage: The Santa Fe Trail and the Mexican War*. Norman: University of Oklahoma Press, 1994.

Charbonneau, Dominique M. *Dictionnaire des Mariages Charbonneau*. Québec: Roger et Jean Bergeron, Bibliotheque Nationale du Québec, 1973.

Chittenden, Hiram Martin. *History of The American Fur Trade of the Far West*. Stanford: Academic Reprints, 1954.

Chuinard, E. G. *Only One Man Died: The Medical Aspects of the Lewis and Clark Expedition*. Glendale, Calif.: Arthur H. Clark Company, 1979.

Clark, Charles G. *The Men of the Lewis and Clark Expedition: A Biographical Roster of the Fifty-one Members and a Composite Diary of Their Activities from All Known Sources*. Glendale, Calif.: Arthur H. Clark Company, 1970.

Clark, William. "Abstract of Expenditures as Superintendent of Indian Affairs, 1823." In *American State Papers*. Washington, D. C.: Gales & Seaton, 1832–61. Microfilm.

Cleary, Rita "Charbonneau Reconsidered." *We Proceeded On* 26 (February 2000): 18–23.

Cleland, R. G. *This Restless Breed of Men: Trappers of the Southwest*. New York: Alfred A. Knopf, Inc., 1950.

Coe, Lewis. *The Telegraph: A History of Morse's Invention and Its Predecessors in the United States*. Jefferson, NC: McFarland, 1993.

Cohen, Yehudi A., ed. *Social Structure and Personality: A Casebook*. New York: Holt, Rinehart and Winston, 1961.

Colby, Susan M. *With Sword, With Cross, With Plough, Stories of Our French Canadian Ancestors*. Self-published, 2000.

———. "Captives of the French and Indian Wars Part 2: Captured from New France." *Michigan's Habitant Heritage: Journal of the French-Canadian Heritage Society of Michigan* 24, no. 3 (July 2003): 133–140.

Cooke, Phillip St. George. "Journal of the March of the Mormon Battalion, 1846–1847." In Ralph P. Bieber, ed., *Exploring Southwestern Trails*. Southwest Historical Series, vol. 7. Glendale, Calif.: Arthur H. Clark Company, 1938.

———. *The Conquest of New Mexico and California, an Historical and Personal Narrative*. 1878. Reprint, Albuquerque: Horn & Wallace, 1964.

Cooley, C. H. *Human Nature and the Social Order*. New York: Charles Scribner's Sons, 1902.

Coues, Elliott, ed. *The History of the Lewis and Clark Expedition, By Meriwether Lewis and William Clark*. 1893. Reprint. New York: Dover, 1965.

Dary, David. *The Santa Fe Trail: Its History, Legends and Lore*. New York: Penguin, 2002.

DeVoto, Bernard. *Across the Wide Missouri*. Boston: Houghton Mifflin, 1964.

Drumm, Stella, ed. *Journal of a Fur-Trading Expedition on the Upper Missouri 1812–1813, by John C. Luttig*. St. Louis: Missouri Historic Society, 1920.

———. *Down the Santa Fe Trail and Into Mexico: The Diary of Susan Shelby Magoffin 1846–47*. Reprint, Lincoln: University of Nebraska Press, 1982.

Drummond, William Henry. *The Voyageur and Other Poems*. New York: G. P. Putnam's Sons, 1905.

Dunham, Harold H. "Ceran St. Vrain." In L. R. Hafen, ed. *Mountain Men and Fur Traders of the Far West*. Lincoln: University of Nebraska Press (1982): 146–165.

Durham, Michael S. *Desert Between the Mountains: Mormons, Miners, Padres, Mountain Men, and the Opening of the Great Basin 1772–1869*. New York: Henry Holt, 1997.

Easton, David, and Robert D. Hess "The Child's Political World." *Midwest Journal of Political Science* 6 (1961): 229–246.

Eder, Jeanne. Public lecture (April 13, 2000). Water Resources Education Center, Vancouver, Wash.

Elliot, T. C. "Journal of John Work." *Oregon Historical Quarterly* 13 (December 1912): 368–70.

Erikson, Erik. *Childhood and Society.* New York: Norton W.W. & Co., 1950.

Faherty, William Barnaby, S.J. *Dream by the River, Two Centuries of Saint Louis Catholicism 1766–1967.* St. Louis: Piraeus, 1973.

———. *The Saint Louis Portrait.* Tulsa: Continental Heritage, 1978.

Faulkner, Ann L. "A Tribute to Alphonse Sierens: 3 Feb 1929–9 Nov 2001." *Michigan's Habitant Heritage: Journal of the French-Canadian Heritage Society of Michigan* 23, no. 1 (January 2002): 41–42.

Ferris, Warren Angus. *Life in the Rocky Mountains, 1830–1835.* Reprint, Salt Lake City: Rocky Mountain Book Shop, 1940.

Flint, Timothy. *Recollections of the Last Ten Years in the Valley of the Mississippi.* 1826. Reprint, Carbondale: Southern Illinois University Press, 1968.

Frazier, Joseph B. "Charbonneau saw world, worked in many trades." *The Columbian* (April 19, 2002).

Frémont, John Charles. *Report of the Exploring Expedition to the Rocky Mountains In the Year 1842, and to Oregon and North California In the Years 1843–'44.* 1845. Reprint, Ann Arbor: University Microfilms, 1966.

Furtwangler, Albert. "Sacagawea's Son as a Symbol." *Oregon Historical Quarterly* 102, no. 3 (Fall 2001): 290–315.

———. "Sacagawea's Son: New Evidence from Germany." *Oregon Historical Quarterly* 102, no. 4 (Winter 2001): 518–523.

Gagné, Peter. "Toussaint Charbonneau." *Connecticut Maple Leaf* 9, no. 4 (2000–1): 224–227.

Gareau, G. Robert. *Premiers Concessions d'Habitations de Boucherville en 1673.* 1973, Montreal. Reprint, Woonsocket, RI: Livre # HIS 214, American French Genealogical Society, 1973.

Gowans, Fred R. *Rocky Mountain Rendezvous: A History of the Fur Trade Rendezvous 1825–1840.* Layton, Utah: Gibbs M. Smith, 1985.

Greenstein, Fred I. *Children and Politics.* New Haven: Yale University Press, 1965.

Grinnell, Calvin. "Another View of Sakakawea." *We Proceeded On* (May 1999): 15–19.

Hafen, Ann W. "Jean-Baptiste Charbonneau." In L. R. Hafen, ed. *French Fur Traders and Voyageurs in the American West.* Lincoln: University of Nebraska Press (1997): 76–95.

Hafen, LeRoy R., ed. *The Mountain Men and the Fur Trade of the Far West.* 10 volumes. Glendale, Calif.: Arthur H. Clark Company, 1965.

———. *Mountain Men and Fur Traders of the Far West.* Lincoln: University of Nebraska Press, 1982.

———. *French Fur Traders and Voyageurs in the American West.* Lincoln: University of Nebraska Press, 1997.

Hafen, LeRoy R., and Ann W. Hafen, eds. *To the Rockies and Oregon, 1839–1842.* Glendale, Calif.: Arthur H. Clark Company, 1955.

Haines, Aubrey L., ed. *Journal of a Trapper: A Hunter's Rambles Among the Wild Regions of the Rocky Mountains, 1834–1843, Osborne Russell.* New York: MJF Books, 1955.

Havard, Giles. *The Great Peace of Montreal of 1701: French-Native Diplomacy in the Seventeenth Century.* Trans. by Phyllis Aronoff and Howard Scott. Montreal and Kingston: McGill-Queen's University Press, 2001.

Hebard, Grace R. *Sacajawea, a Guide and Interpreter of the Lewis and Clark Expedition, with an Account of the Travels of Toussaint Charonneau, and of Jean Baptiste, The Expedition Papoose.* Glendale, Calif.: Arthur H. Clark Company, 1932.

Hoffhaus, Charles E. "French Made Lewis and Clark Expedition Successful." *Kansas City Star* (October 10, 13, and 18, 1980).

Howard, Harold P. *Sacajawea.* Norman: University of Oklahoma Press, 1971.

Howard, Helen Addison. "The Puzzle of Baptiste Charbonneau." *Journal of San Diego History* 2, no. 2 (April 1965): 10–12, 50–53.

Hunsaker, Joyce Badgley. *Sacagawea Speaks: Beyond the Shining Mountains with Lewis and Clark.* Guilford, Conn.: The Globe Pequot Press, 2001.

Huser, Verne. "On the Rivers with Lewis and Clark." *We Proceeded On* (May 2003): 17–24.

Hussey, John A., ed. *Early Sacramento: Glimpses of John Augustus Sutter, The Hok Farm and Neighboring Indian Tribes from the journals of Prince Paul H.R.H. Duke Paul Wilhelm of Württemberg.* Translated by Louis Butscher. Sacramento: The Sacramento Book Collectors Club, 1973.

Inman, Henry. *The Old Santa Fe Trail, The Story of a Great Highway.* New York: MacMillan, 1897.

Irving, Washington. *The Adventures of Captain Bonneville.* New York: G.P. Putnam, 1859.

———. *Captain Bonneville.* Portland: Binforts and Mort, 1972

Jackson, Donald, ed. *Letters of the Lewis and Clark Expedition, with Related Documents, 1783–1854.* 2d ed., 2 vols. Urbana: University of Illinois Press, 1978.

Jennings, J. D. *Prehistory of North America.* 2d ed. New York: McGraw-Hill, 1974.

Kennerly, William Clark, with Elizabeth Russell. *Persimmon Hill: A Narrative of Old St. Louis and the Far West.* Norman: University of Oklahoma Press, 1948.

King, Edith W., and August Kerber. *The Sociology of Early Childhood Education.* New York: American Book Co., 1966.

Kubik, Barbara J. "Sacagawea." Public lecture (January 24, 2002). City of Vancouver Heritage Lecture Series. Marshall House, Vancouver, Wash.

Lange, Robert E. "Poor Charbonneau! Was He As Incompetent As The Journals/Narratives Make Him Out To Be?" *We Proceeded On* 6 (May 1980): 14–16.

Lardner, W. B., and M. J. Brock. *History of Placer and Nevada Counties California.* Los Angeles: Historic Record Company, 1924.

Lecompte, Janet. "Pierre Chouteau, Junior." In L. R. Hafen, ed. *Mountain Men and Fur Traders of the Far West.* Lincoln: University of Nebraska Press (1982): 24–56.

Madsen, Bringham D. *Lemhi: Sacajawea's People.* Caldwell, Idaho: The Caxton Printers, 1978.

Mattison, Ray H. "The Upper Missouri Fur Trade: Its Methods of Operation." Reprint *Nebraska History* 42, no. 1 (March 1961): 1–27.

McLeod, Norman. "Heritage: Jean Baptiste Charbonneau, Cultured Mountain Man." *Sierra Heritage* (Fall 1983): 20–23.

McNitt, Frank. *The Indian Traders*. Norman: University of Oklahoma Press, 1962.

Mead, G. H. *Mind, Self and Society, From the Standpoint of a Social Behaviorist*. Part 3. Chicago: University of Chicago Press, 1934.

Moore, Bob. "Pompey's Baptism, A recently discovered document sheds light on the christening of Jean Baptiste Charbonneau." *We Proceeded On* 26 (February 2000): 11–17.

Morgan, Dale L., and Eleanor Towles Harris, eds. *The Rocky Mountain Journals of William Marshall Anderson—The West in 1834*. Reprint, San Marino, Calif.: The Huntington Library, 1967.

Morin, Gaëtan, ed. *Programme de recherche en démographie historique (PRDH)*. Database by Hubert Charbonneau and Jacques Légaré. Montréal: Université de Montréal, Dept. de Demographie.

Moulton, Gary E., ed. *The Journals of the Lewis and Clark Expedition*. 13 volumes. Lincoln: University of Nebraska Press, 1986–2001.

Munnick, Harriet D. "Jean Baptiste Lucier, dit Gardipe." In L. R. Hafen, ed. *French Fur Traders and Voyageurs in the American West*. Lincoln: University of Nebraska Press (1997): 208–216.

Murphy, Robert F., and Yolanda. "Shoshone-Bannock Subsistence and Society." *Anthropological Records* 16, no. 7, Department of the Interior. Berkeley: University of California Press, 1960.

Mussulman, Joseph. "Pomp's bier was a bar." *We Proceeded On* 27, no. 1 (February 2001): 39–40.

Nelson, W. Dale. *Interpreters with Lewis and Clark: The Story of Sacagawea and Toussaint Charbonneau*. Denton: University of North Texas Press, 2003.

Nitske, W. R., trans., and Savoie Lottinville, ed. *Paul Wilhelm von Württemberg, Travels in North America 1822–24*. Norman: University of Oklahoma Press, 1970.

Nute, Grace Lee. *The Voyageur*. Reprint edition. St. Paul: Minnesota Historical Society, 1955.

Oglesby, Richard E. *Manuel Lisa and the Opening of the Missouri Fur Trade*. Norman: University of Oklahoma Press, 1963.

Ottoson, Dennis R. "Toussaint Charbonneau, A Most Durable Man." *South Dakota History* 6, no. 2 (Spring 1976): 152–85.

Owen, Roger C., James J. F. Deetz, and Anthony D. Fisher. *The North American Indians: A Sourcebook*. New York: Macmillan Publishing, 1967.

Parkman, Francis. *The Oregon Trail*. Garden City, NY: International Collectors Library, 1945.

Peabody, George W. "'Pomp' is First Baby Ever on a U.S. Coin." *California Historian* (Summer 2000): 8–17.

Phillips, Paul C., ed. *W. A. Ferris, Life in the Rocky Mountains*. Denver: F. A. Rosenstock, Old West Publishing Company, 1940.

Piaget, Jean. *The Language and Thought of the Child*. New York: Harcourt, Brace & Co., 1963.

Porter, Mae Reed, and Odessa Davenport. *Scotsman in Buckskin*. New York: Hastings House, 1963.

Reps, John W. *Cities on the Mississippi: Nineteenth Century Images of Urban Development*. Columbia: University of Missouri Press, 1994.

Ricketts, Norma Baldwin. *The Morman Battalion: U.S. Army of the West*. Logan: Utah State University Press, 1996.

Ronda, James P. *Lewis and Clark among the Indians*. Lincoln: University of Nebraska Press, 1984.

Rogers, Ann. *Lewis and Clark in Missouri*. Third edition. Columbia: University of Missouri Press, 2002.

———. *Life in the Far West*. Norman: University of Oklahoma Press, 1951. Originally published in *Blackwood's Edinburgh Magazine* (June 1848).

Sage, Rufus B. *Rocky Mountain Life*. 1846. Reprint, 1982. Lincoln: University of Nebraska Press.

Sampson, William R. "Nathaniel Jarvis Wyeth." In L. R. Hafen, ed. *Mountain Men and Fur Traders of the Far West*. Lincoln: University of Nebraska Press (1982): 311–331.

Sanborn, Dorothy, ed. *Chronology of Auburn, California 1848 to 1910*. Revised edition. Vol. 1 (January 2001). Auburn, Calif.: Auburn Sesquicentennial Research Committee.

Schierle, Sonja, ed. *Travels in the Interior of North America*. Köln: Taschen, 2001.

Schultz, James Willard. *Bird Woman*. Boston: Houghton Mifflin, 1918.

Sharbono, Tom. "History of the Charbonneau (Sharbono) Families. Descendents of Oliver Charbonneau and Marie Marguerite Garnier, Morans France." Unpublished papers on file at Placer County Library, Auburn, Calif.

Shepard, Elihu H. *The Early History of St. Louis and Missouri: Its First Exploration by White Men in 1673 to 1843*. St. Louis: Southwestern Book and Publishing, 1870.

Slaughter, Thomas. *Exploring Lewis and Clark: Reflections on Men and Wilderness*. New York: Alfred A. Knopf, 2003.

Smith, E. Willard. "Journal." In L. R. Hafen and Ann W. Hafen, eds. *To the Rockies and Oregon, 1939–1842*. The Far West and Rockies Series, vol. 3. Glendale, Calif.: Arthur H. Clark Company, 1955.

Speck, Gordon. *Breeds and Half-Breeds*. New York: Clarkson N. Potter, 1969.

Steffen, Jerome O. *William Clark: Jeffersonian Man on the Frontier*. Norman: University of Oklahoma Press, 1977.

Sublette Papers, Missouri Historical Society.

Sunder, John E. *Bill Sublette: Mountain Man*. Norman: University of Oklahoma Press, 1959.

Swagerty, William R. "Marriage and Settlement Patterns of Rocky Mountain Trappers and Traders." *Western Historical Quarterly* 11 (April 1980): 159–80.

Swanton, John R. *The Indian Tribes of North America*. Smithsonian Institution Bureau of American Ethnology Bulletin # 145. Washington, D.C.: Smithsonian Institution Press, 1984.

Talbot, Margaret. "Searching for Sacagawea." *National Geographic* (February 2003): 68–85.

Thomasma, Kenneth. *The Truth About Sacajawea*. Jackson, Wyo.: Grandview Publishing, 1997.

Thwaites, Reuben Gold, ed. *Original Journals of the Lewis and Clark Expedition, 1804–1806*. Reprint (1904–1907). 7 volumes and atlas. New York: Arno Press, 1969.

———. "Farnham, Farnham's Travels." *Early Western Travels* 28 (1904–7).

———. "Maximilian, Prince of Wied, Travels in the Interior of North America." *Early Western Travels* 22–24 (1904–1907).

Tinling, Marion. *Sacagawea's Son: The Life of Jean Baptiste Charbonneau*, Missoula, Mont.: Mountain Press, 2001.

Tobie, Harvey E. "Joseph L. Meek." In Leroy R. Hafen, ed. *Mountain Men and Fur Traders of the Far West*. Lincoln: University of Nebraska Press (1982): 346–368.

Trenholm, Virginia Cole and Maurine Carley. *Shoshonis: Sentinels of the Rockies*. Norman: University of Oklahoma Press, 1964.

Tyler, Sergeant Daniel. *A Concise History of The Mormon Battalion in the Mexican War 1846–1847*. 2d printing. Glorieta, NM: The Rio Grande Press, 1969.

Vaillancourt, Jacques. "Sacagawea 1790–1812." *L'Ancêtre* 28, no. 1 (2001): 37–39.

Van Kirk, Sylvia. *Many Tender Ties: Women in the Fur Trade Society, 1670–1870*. Norman: University of Oklahoma Press, 1980.

Vestal, Stanley. *Jim Bridger Mountain Man*. Lincoln: University of Nebraska Press, 1970.

Victor, Frances Fuller. *The River of the West: Life and Adventure in the Rocky Mountains and Oregon*. Hartford, Conn.: Columbus Book Company, 1870.

Von Sachsen-Altenburg, Hans, and Robert L. Dyer. *Duke Paul of Wuerttemberg on the Missouri Frontier 1823, 1830 and 1851*. Booneville, Mo.: Pekitanoui Publications, Boonville, 1998.

Waldman, Carl. *Biographical Dictionary of American Indian History to 1900*. Revised edition. New York: Checkmark Books, 2001.

Wheeler, Olin D. *The Trail of Lewis and Clark, 1804–1806*. 2 volumes. New York: G. P. Putnam's Sons, 1904.

Wilson, Elinor. *Jim Beckwourth: Black Mountain Man and War Chief of the Crows*. Norman: University of Oklahoma Press, 1972.

Woodworth, James K., and William G. Wilson. "Murderer's Bar: A Name from History." *Rivers of Gold*. Placer Savings and Loan Association. Undated ms. on file at the Auburn Placer County Library.

Index

Abert, James W., 18, 154
Alvarado, Johann (Juan), 107
American Fur Company. *See* fur companies; Charbonneau, Jean-Baptiste
American River, 48, 164, 165, 166, 167, 168, 171, 173, 175
Anderson, William Marshall, 133*n*.43, 136–37, 138
Auburn (Placer County), Calif., 18, 48, 163, 164, 165–66, 168, 172–75

beaver. *See* fur trade
Beckwourth, James, 17, 115, 146–47, 164, 165, 167, 173, 175, 176–77, 179
Bent, Charles and William, 140–41, 142, 146, 156, 164
Bent's Fort. *See* Forts
Boggs, William M., 114, 153–54, 177
Boone family, 97, 130
Bridger, Jim, 17, 116, 127, 128, 130–32, 133*n*.43, 136, 138, 139, 175, 176, 179
Buckner, Tom, 165, 166, 177, 179
buffalo (bison). *See* fur trade

Cahokia Mounds, 83–84, 85; photo of, 85
California, 18, 156, 157, 159–76, 182
Cameahwait, 38, 47, 58
Carson, Kit, 33*n*.25, 114–15*n*.6, 138, 145, 147–48

Catholicism, 23, 72–73, 80, 90, 92–93
Charbonneau, Jean-Baptiste (grandfather), 15, 22, 24*n*.7, 25, 26, 183–84
Charbonneau, Jean-Baptiste: as alcalde, 18, 159–62, 181; and American Fur Company, 122, 124, 127–32, 134–35, 141, 154; appearance of, 29–31, 114, 116–17, 127, 154, 158; baptism of, 16, 72–73, 82, 184; birth of, 16, 19–20, 184; as cart driver, 18, 149–51; character/values of, 68, 70, 77, 102, 113–14, 137, 149, 161, 163–64*n*.2, 172, 176–78, 182; and Charbonneau, Toussaint (father), 49, 55–56, 64–65, 71–72, 79, 89–91, 98–99, 105–6, 117, 138*n*.52, 151; and Corps of Discovery, 20, 49, 53, 54–65, 176, 179; dancing of, 61–62, 64, 68–70, 136–37, 179; death of, 18, 174*n*.25, 175–76, 179–81, 184; and Duke Paul of Württemberg, 17, 29–31, 103–12, 169–72, 177, 178*n*.30; education of, 64, 65–66, 76–77, 90, 92–94, 98–99, 101, 103, 105–6, 109–10, 113, 114, 115, 142–43, 147, 149, 161, 178, 179, 181; and Enlightenment, 65–67, 182; in Europe, 17, 105, 106, 108–111, 142, 149, 175, 176, 181, 182; genealogy of, 22–25, 183–84; and gold rush, 18, 162–69, 172, 175, 181; as guide, 18, 115, 120,

157–58, 175, 181; as Hidatsa boy, 68–70, 76; historic marker of, 18, 180–81; in hotel business, 18, 164–65, 166–67, 173; as hunter, 18, 110, 115, 143–44, 145–46, 149–51, 158, 175, 176; illnesses of, 16, 60–61, 175, 179, 181; as Indian, 58, 68–70, 76, 115, 116–19, 127, 136–37, 163, 173, 174n.25, 177, 178, 182; as multilingual/interpreter, 93, 105–6, 109–10, 113, 115, 120, 136, 149, 157, 159, 175, 181; as métis, 10–12, 31, 33, 77, 84, 99, 113, 114, 115, 119, 136–37, 142–43, 149, 154, 161–62, 177, 178, 182; and Mormon Battalion, 18, 157–59, 175; as Mountain Man, 113–38, 172, 181; offspring of, 110–11, 148, 148–49n.17; 154, 172, 184n.11; personality of, 20, 61, 64, 76–77, 107, 113–14, 115, 149, 151, 158, 163, 176–77; as "Pomp," 62, 64, 71, 88; possible drawing of, 30; and racism, 84, 99, 161–62, 172; return from Europe of, 17, 111–12, 181; and Sacagawea (mother), 19–20, 49, 52–53, 54–56, 58–61, 68, 71–75, 78, 79, 109, 151, 176–77; in St. Louis, Mo., 17, 18, 71–99, 108, 112, 151, 153; sense of humor of, 113, 147, 149; skills of, 110, 114–15; 121–22, 128; 136–37; 143–44, 146, 149, 154, 155, 157, 158–59; and Spanish Southwest, 17, 138, 140–49, 153–62; as symbol, 67, 106, 178–79, 181, 182; and Upper Missouri fur trade, 17, 101, 103–4, 112, 115, 122, 124–38; as ward of William Clark, 64–65, 73, 75, 88–89, 94, 97, 99, 103, 105, 122, 142–43, 150–51, 176–77, 178n.30, 181. *See also* Clark, William

Charbonneau, Lizette, 16, 79, 86–87, 88, 90–91, 92
Charbonneau, Michel (great-great-grandfather), 24–26, 183, 184
Charbonneau, Michel (great-grandfather), 25, 183, 184
Charbonneau, Olivier, 22–24, 26, 183, 184
Charbonneau, Toussaint: and American Fur Company, 27; appearance of, 28, 29, 117; birth of, 15, 22, 25, 184; character/values of, 31–36, 53, 58, 63–64, 72, 74–75, 87, 152; and Jean-Baptiste, 19, 71, 72, 89, 98, 105–6, 115, 117, 138n.52; as cook, 53, 56, 152; and Corps of Discovery, 16, 21–22, 24n.8, 31–32, 49, 51, 53, 56, 63–64, 71, 73–74, 104, 150, 153n.23, 154, 159; death of, 18, 151, 153, 184; and Duke Paul of Württemberg, 98, 104–5; employment by U.S. Indian Department Upper Missouri sub-agency, 17, 98, 152–53; as farmer, 16, 65, 67, 74–75, 76; at Fort Clark, 17, 34, 152; at Fort Kiowa, 104; at Fort Manuel, 85–88; at Fort Pembina, 16, 27; as fur trader, 26–27, 35, 36, 47, 76, 89, 98, 123–24; heritage of, 22–25, 36, 183, 184; and Hidatsa, 15, 27, 76, 104, 152, as illiterate, 115n.7; as interpreter, 22, 27, 32, 35, 51, 53, 58, 63, 70n.36, 98, 104, 133, 149, 152; and Manuel Lisa, 16, 74–76, 79, 123–24; as missing, 17, 89, 139–40, 152; and North West Fur Company, 15, 26; offspring of, 88, 91, 152n.22; at Pine Fort, 26–27; possible drawing of, 29; and Sacagawea, 19, 32, 34, 36–37, 40–43, 47, 52, 55–58, 74–75, 76, 85–86, 183; at

St. Louis, Mo., 71–74, 76, 80; and Spanish Southwest, 89, 139–40; and Prince Maximilian, 28–29, 32, 33, 35, 70*n*.36, 98, 132–33; and women, 32, 34, 52, 152. *See also* Clark, William

Chouteau, Auguste: as civic leader, 72–73, 84, 96, 97; as founder of St. Louis, 15, 72, 79; as fur trade mogul, 89, 101, 103, 123, 124; as godfather of Jean-Baptiste, 72–73, 81, 84, 150, 178*n*.30

Clark, George Rogers, 105, 123

Clark, Jefferson Kennerly, 97, 150, 151

Clark, Julia (Judith) Hancock, 77, 91, 92, 96, 97

Clark, Meriwether Lewis, 91–92, 159

Clark, William: background of, 105; at Big Bones Lick, Ky., 105; and Charbonneau, Toussaint, 32, 36, 63–65, 67, 73, 74, 75, 98, 104, 123, 151–52, 159; and Corps of Discovery, 19, 50–53, 55–56, 58–67, 123, 159; death of, 17, 95*n*.44, 152; and Duke Paul of Württemberg, 103–5, 106, 112; and education, 67, 92–94, 105; and Enlightenment, 65–67, 84–85, 91, 92, 97, 102, 103, 106, 123; and fur trade, 84, 122–23, 124, 142; as governor, 17, 92, 96, 97–98, 123; as Jean-Baptiste's guardian, 64–65, 73, 75, 84, 88–89, 94, 97, 99, 103–4, 105, 122, 142–43, 150, 176–77, 178, 181; and Jean-Baptiste prior to guardianship, 19, 55–56, 58–62, 64-65, 67, 71, 72*n*.3; and Indian affairs, 66–67, 81, 85, 95, 97–98, 151, 161, 178; marriage and family of, 43*n*.52, 77–78, 90–92, 96–97, 150–51; museum of, 96, 141; and Sacagawea, 40, 56, 58, 60, 64, 67, 75, 159; and St. Louis, 50, 73–79, 81, 84, 89–99; sense of humor of, 62, 147; and Shoshoni, 44

Columbia Fur Company. *See* fur companies

Cooke, Phillip St. George, 114, 117, 157, 158, 159

Corps of Discovery, 16, 20, 21, 28, 38, 43, 48, 49–70, 71, 73, 120, 121, 143, 181, 182

Deniau, Marguerite, 22, 25

Donner, Oregon. *See* Inskip's Station

Drips, Andrew, 124–25, 126, 128, 130, 131, 134, 136, 137. *See also* fur companies, American Fur Company

Drouillard, George, 24*n*.8, 28, 53, 55, 121

DuBourg, Bp. Louis W. V., 93–94

education, 92–94, 161. *See also* Charbonneau, Jean-Baptise; St. Louis Academy

Enlightenment, 65–66, 102–3, 106, 123, 132–33, 178, 182. *See also* Charbonneau, Jean-Baptise; Clark, William

Farnham, T. J., 118, 145

Ferris, Warren A., 112, 125*n*.29, 130

Fitzpatrick, Thomas, 18, 126–27, 129, 131, 135, 136, 154–55. *See also* fur companies, Rocky Mountain Fur Company

Fontenelle, Lucien, 124–25, 126, 129, 130, 134, 136, 137, 139. *See also* fur companies, American Fur Company

forts: Bent's Fort, 17, 18, 48, 118,

139–41, 145, 146, 148, 153–54, 155, 156, 164; Fort Clark, 17, 34, 48, 112, 152; Fort Clatsop, 48, 60; Fort Kiowa, 104; Fort Mandan, 16, 20–22, 48, 181, 184, photo of, 21; Fort Manuel, 48, 85–88, 90; Fort Pembina, 16, 27; Fort Union, 48, 112, 129; Fort Vasquez, 48, 142, 145; Pine Fort, 26–27
Frémont, John C., 17, 33*n*.25, 118, 147
French/French Canadian, 22–28, 33, 35–36, 94, 117–18, 119, 141, 142, 148, 172, 175, 182, 183, 184
fur companies: American Fur Company, 27, 122, 124, 127–32, 134–35, 136, 139, 141, 154; Columbia Fur Company, 124; Hudson's Bay Company, 124, 126, 128, 134; Missouri Fur Company, 16, 84, 98, 101, 123, 124; North West Fur Company, 15, 24, 26, 27, 33*n*.28, 124, 184*n*.7; Rocky Mountain Fur Company, 124, 125, 127, 128, 129–30, 134, 136, 154; St. Louis Fur Company, 123, 134
fur trade: as to attire, 116–17; as to beaver skins, 120, 139, 140; as to buffalo (bison), 120, 140, 143–44, 145–46; and Charbonneau heritage, 23–28; importance of, 50–51, 66, 120; in Montreal, 23–25, 80; and polygamy, 34; in St. Louis, 80, 84, 97, 122–24, 127, 142; in Southwest, 89, 138, 139–62; in Upper Missouri/Rocky Mountains, 115–40. *See also* Forts; Fur Companies
Fur Trappers. *See* Mountain Men; names of individuals

Gass, Patrick, 19, 182, 184*n*.11
Gaultier de Varennes, Pierre (Chevalier, Sieur de la Verendrye), 15, 24*n*.8
Gold Rush, 18, 162, 163–76
Green River. *See* Rendezvous

Ham's Fork. *See* Rendezvous
Hudson's Bay Company. *See* Fur Companies
Hunter, Jesse, 160, 161, 162

Indians, 33, 41, 54, 66–67, 76, 81, 83–84, 87, 95, 97–99, 119, 161, 163–64*n*.2, 171. *See also* Indian Tribes
Indian tribes: Apache, 140, 157; Arapaho, 39, 140; Arikara (Ree), 71, 87, 104, 121; Atsena, 130; Blackfoot, 15, 39, 42, 121, 130, 131, 138, 139, 154, 177; Cherokee, 95*n*.44, 173; Cheyenne, 39, 87, 140, 148, 154; Comanche, 127, 155; Crow, 36, 164, 175, 176–77; Delaware, 81; Flathead, 38, 141; Hidatsa (Minataree, Gros Ventre), 15, 20, 22, 27*n*.11, 32, 36, 39–43, 45–47, 51, 54*n*.10, 58, 62, 68–70, 76, 77, 87, 104, 107, 133, 152; Iroquois, 23, 25; Jicarill, 140; Kansas, 31, 104, 106*n*.10, 107; Maidu, 167; Mandan, 15, 20, 21, 27*n*.11, 45, 63, 68, 69, 77, 112, 152*n*.23; Mountain Ute, 140; Nez Perce, 38, 59, 107, 130, 141; Osage, 81; Pawnee, 127, 143; Renard, 81; Sac, 81; Shawnee, 81; Shoshoni (Lemhi), 15, 22, 36–39, 43–46, 51–52, 54*n*.10, 56–58, 134, 170, 177; Sioux, 25*n*.9, 39, 151
individual versus community values, 95, 97. *See also* Enlightenment

Index

Inskip's Station, 18, 48, 180, 181, 184

Jefferson, Thomas, 49–52, 65–66, 95, 105, 122–23. *See also* Enlightenment
Jessaume, René, 19, 22, 67, 87, 90
Jessaume, Toussaint, 67, 78, 88*n*.29, 90–91
Joliet, Louis, 15, 27

Kearny, Steven Watts, 155–56, 157
Kennerly, William Clark, 113–14, 150
Kennett, William Clark, 150

Lewis and Clark. *See* Corps of Discovery; Lewis, Meriwether; Clark, William
Lewis, Meriwether: and Blackfoot, 121; and Charbonneau, Jean-Baptiste, 19, 61, 184*n*.11; and Charbonneau, Toussaint, 32, 63; and Corps of Discovery, 50, 51, 52, 55, 58, 61, 63, 65, 66, 86, 142; death of, 16, 78, 91; and Jessaume, Toussaint, 67, 78, 90–91; and Sacagawea, 19, 42*n*.50, 86; in St. Louis, 50, 77–78; as scholar, 105; and Shoshoni, 44–45
Liguest, Pierre Laclede, 15, 72, 79
Lisa, Manuel, 16, 74–76, 79, 84, 85, 121, 123–24
Louisiana Purchase, 16, 27–28, 48, 49–51
Luttig, John, 86–89

Mackensie, Alexander, 15, 50
Marquette, Jacques, 15, 27
Maximilian of Wied-Neuwied, Prince, 28–29, 32, 33, 35, 70*n*.36, 98, 132–33

Meek, Joe, 17, 115–16, 126–27
métis, 10, 11, 12, 22, 31, 67, 84, 115, 128, 130, 136–37, 171–72. *See also* Charbonneau, Jean-Baptiste
Mexican War, 92, 154, 155, 159, 175
Mexico, 17, 124, 142, 155, 160, 170. *See also* Mexican War; Santa Fe Trail
Mission San Luis Rey, 18, 48, 159–61, 179; drawing of, 160
missionaries. *See* Whitman, Marcus
Missouri Fur Company. *See* fur companies
Möllhausen, Heinrich, 30*n*.15, 106
Monk's Mound. *See* Cahokia Mounds
Montreal, 22–27, 72, 80–81, 83, 151*n*.19
Mormon Battalion/Trail, 18, 48, 155–57, 160, 162, 175, 176, 179
Mountain Man, 113–38, 156, 165, 172. *See also* Charbonneau, Jean-Baptiste
Murderer's Bar, 48, 164, 165*n*.7, 166–69, 173*n*.21

New Madrid earthquakes, 78–79
New Mexico, 38, 140–41, 155, 158. *See also* Santa Fe Trail
New Orleans, 27, 48, 103, 108, 112, 170, 172
North Dakota, 15, 16, 20, 27, 86
North West Fur Company. *See* fur companies

Parkman, Francis, 30*n*.16, 33, 42*n*.48, 71, 76, 113, 117, 119, 139, 144*n*.9, 163–64*n*.2, 178
Paul Wilhelm of Württemberg, Duke: 100, background of, 101–3, 105, 106, 109, 132; and Charbonneau, Jean-Baptiste; 17, 29–31,

103–12, 169–72, 177, 178*n*.30; and Charbonneau, Toussaint, 98, 104–5; and Clark, William, 103–5, 106, 112; drawing of, 100; marriage of, 102*n*.4, 110; as to Mergentheim, 100, 110, 111, 169; and other protégés, 107–8, 110, 178*n*.30; in Sacramento area, 18, 169–72
Pierre's Hole. *See* Rendezvous
Pine Fort. *See* forts
Placer Herald (newspaper), 163, 165, 166, 174–76, 177
Platte River/Valley, 48, 118–19, 125, 127, 142, 145, 146, 149, 153, 172
"Pomp." *See* Charbonneau, Jean-Baptiste
Pompey's Pillar. *See* Pompy's Tower
Pompy's Tower, 16, 18, 48, 62–63, 110*n*.20, 147; photo of, 63
Provost, Etienne, 127, 129, 130. *See also* Fur Companies, American Fur Company

Quebec. *See* Montreal

racial/ethnic attitudes, 31–33, 34*n*.31, 35–36, 41, 44, 66, 84, 95, 97, 98, 99, 106–8, 121, 137, 161–62, 165, 170–72, 177, 182
Rendezvous, at Green River, 48, 125, 133–35, 139; at Ham's Fork, 136; at Pierre's Hole, 127–30; at Wind River, 125
Rocky Mountain Fur Company. *See* Fur Companies
Ruxton, George F., 114, 116
Rubidoux Fur Brigade, 17, 112, 124, 125. *See also* Fur Companies, American Fur Company

Sacagawea: abuse of, 32, 34; birth/age of, 15, 39, 42*n*.50; capture of, 15, 36, 37, 39, 42, 182; character/values of, 47, 52–53, 60, 74–75, 86; on coin, 57; and Corps of Discovery, 16, 22, 36, 38, 49, 51, 52, 53, 54–65. 67, 74, 104, 150, 154, 159, 181; death of, 16, 85–86, 88, 124, 161, 174*n*.25, 184; descriptions of, 73, 74–75, 104, 150, 154, 157, 175; heritage of, 36–38, 177, 178; as Hidatsa, 37, 40–43, 45–47, 70; illnesses of, 55, 74–76, 86; image of, 31, 36; as interpreter, 22, 51, 58, 104; and Manuel Lisa, 16, 74–76, 79, 124; as to name, 36*n*.35, 62*n*.29; at Pacific Ocean, 60; in St. Louis, 71–74, 76, 79*n*.14; as Shoshoni, 22, 36–39, 43–46, 51, 56–58, 74, 177; as "slave", 36, 40–42; votes, 59–60; as wife of Toussaint Charbonneau, 19, 32, 34, 36–37, 40–43, 47, 52, 55–58, 74, 75, 76, 79*n*.14, 85–86, 183. *See also* Charbonneau, Jean-Baptiste
Sage, Rufus, 17, 113, 115, 116, 117, 149
St. Louis Academy, 93–94, 109
St. Louis Fur Company. *See* fur companies
St. Louis, Mo.: change at, 50, 81, 95; Charbonneaus as a family at, 16, 71–74, 76; in 1811, 79–85; founding of, 15, 72, 79; and France, 27; and fur trade, 80, 84, 97, 122–24, 127, 142; life in, 96,97; map of, 82; population of, 20, 50, 79, 81, 95, 141; race relations in, 95, 98–99. *See also* Charbonneau, Jean-Baptiste
St. Vrain, Ceran, 140, 141, 142, 146, 153, 156, 164
Santa Fe. *See* Santa Fe Trail

Santa Fe Trail, 17, 48, 117, 124, 138, 139, 141, 142, 149, 153, 155, 156, 164, 179
Smith, E. Willard, 45, 142–43, 145–46
Spanish Southwest. *See* Santa Fe Trail
Stewart, William Drummond (Sir), 133, 149, 153
Sublette, Andrew, 17, 142
Sublette, Milton, 129, 130, 136. *See also* fur companies, Rocky Mountain Fur Company
Sublette, Solomon, 153
Sublette, William, 98, 125, 129, 130, 134, 136, 149, 150, 153. *See also* fur companies, Rocky Mountain Fur Company
Sutter, John, 162, 163, 170, 171

Sutter's Mill (Coloma, Calif.). *See* Sutter, John

Texas, 155, 170
Trappist Monks, 73, 83

Vancouver, George, 15, 59n.20,
Vasquez, Louis, 17, 135, 142
voyageur, 119, 182n.32

War of 1812, 16, 33, 84, 85–88, 92, 95, 98, 124
Warner's Ranch, 48, 159
Whitman, Marcus, 131, 133, 139
Wind River Rendezvous. *See* Rendezvous
Wyeth, Nathaniel, 131–32, 134–35, 179

Sacagawea's Child:
The Life and Times of Jean-Baptiste (Pomp) Charbonneau
by Susan M. Colby
has been produced in an edition of 750 copies.

The typeface used is Caslon.
Design by Ariane C. Smith under the direction of Robert A. Clark.
Printing by Thomson-Shore, Inc., of Dexter, Michigan.